Knowledge of SELF

Middle School Facilitator's Guide

Created by Cedric A. Washington

TM

Executive Director, NERD Youth Services, Inc.

"Speak it. Believe it. Do it."

Knowledge of SELF Curriculum — Middle School Facilitator's Guide

Who Lives Like This?! Publishing LLC
www.nerdyouthservices.org

ISBN: 978-1-970680-12-6 (Paperback)

Cover design and interior layout by
Who Lives Like This?! Publishing LLC Design Team

Printed in the United States of America

First Edition — 2025

Table of Contents

Unit 5   Good People Skills

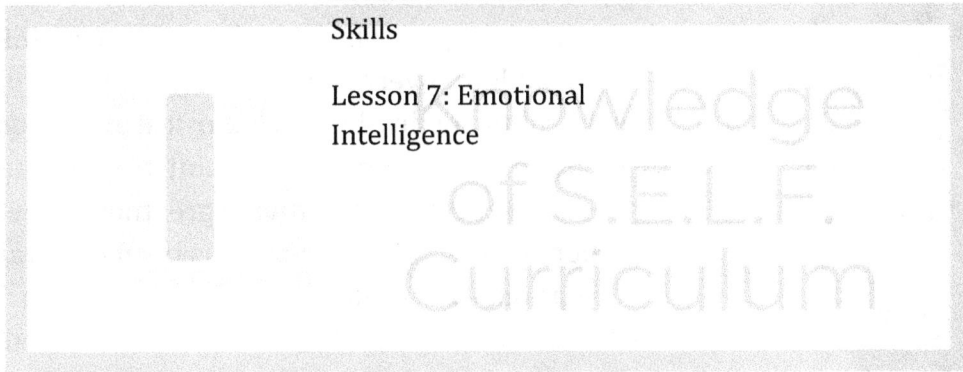

About the Author

Cedric A. Washington is a master educator, speaker, author, former college basketball player, and the Executive Director of NERD Youth Services, Inc. A native of Gary, Indiana. Over two decades of experience in education, mentoring, and community leadership have fueled his commitment to building culturally responsive, empowering programs for African American youth. As the visionary behind the Knowledge of SELF (Social Empowerment Learning Framework) curriculum, Cedric blends historical awareness, emotional intelligence, leadership training, and personal reflection to cultivate greatness in every student he reaches. His work has been celebrated nationally at education conferences, faith institutions, and youth leadership summits. Cedric's mission is simple but powerful: To equip young people with the self-knowledge, discipline, and purpose they need to transform themselves — and the world.

Knowledge of SELF Curriculum

Bonus Tools & Supporting Resources

Middle School, High School, and Young Adult Editions

By Cedric A. Washington

"Speak it. Believe it. Do it."

Daily Affirmations

I AM a trailblazer. I AM destined to succeed. Speak it. Believe it. Do it. – Cedric A. Washington

- I am enough, just as I am.
- My history is powerful, my future is greater.
- I am not what the world calls me—I am who God created me to be.
- I will lead with love, courage, and clarity.
- My skin, my hair, my mind—divinely designed.
- I rise above every label and lie.
- Greatness is not ahead of me; it's within me.
- I walk in wisdom and purpose.
- I am part of a legacy of excellence.
- I build, I uplift, I transform.

Icebreaker Activity Bank

Identity Shields

Students draw a shield divided into 4 parts: family, culture, goals, and values.

Affirmation Circle

Each student shares one positive word about themselves. Then peers affirm each person.

If You Really Knew Me

In a safe circle, students complete the sentence: 'If you really knew me, you'd know...'

Who's in Your Circle?

Draw a circle of influence. Identify family, friends, mentors who shape your SELF.

Two Truths and a Dream

Students share two true things about themselves and one aspirational goal.

Pre-Reflection Survey

Before starting the Knowledge of SELF curriculum, please answer honestly:

1. What do you currently know about your cultural identity?

2. How confident are you in making positive decisions for your future? (1–5)

3. What does success mean to you?

4. Have you ever felt misunderstood in school or in life? Explain.

5. What do you hope to gain from this experience?

Post-Reflection Survey

After completing the Knowledge of SELF curriculum, reflect on the following:

1. What is something new you learned about yourself?

2. How has your definition of success changed?

3. What parts of your identity do you embrace more now than before?

4. What are three personal goals you now feel ready to achieve?

5. How will you use what you've learned to uplift others?

Certificate of Completion

This certifies that

_____

has successfully completed the

Knowledge of SELF Curriculum

Middle School / High School / Young Adult Edition

Led by: _____

Date: _____

Created by Cedric A. Washington | "Speak it. Believe it. Do it."

TM

Knowledge of SELF Middle School Facilitator's Guide ™

Unit 1: SELF CONSCIENCE

Lesson 1: Am I a Color? (Part 1)

Objective:
Students will begin to question identity labels and explore the difference between *ethnic identity* and *national identity* in a way they can clearly understand.

Do Now (Student Prompt):
Do you recognize yourself as African American? If yes, what does that mean to you? If no, how do you describe yourself?
(Students write 3–5 sentences.)

Facilitator's Talk (Guided Script):
Explain to students that for a long time, people have used labels like *Nigger, Negro, Colored, Black, African American* to describe our people. Tell them these labels didn't start with us and often caused **confusion, shame, and broken identity**.

Share with them:

- Some labels were given to us during slavery and Jim Crow to control how we saw ourselves.
- Many of us have been told what we are, but not **who** we are or **where** we come from.

Then introduce two key ideas and write them on the board:

- **Ethnicity** – Your cultural identity, traditions, and roots (for example: Igbo, Yoruba, Haitian, Jamaican, etc.).
- **Nationality** – The nation (country) you are a citizen of (for example: American, Jamaican, Nigerian).

Explain that many of our students call themselves "African American" but have never been told what country in Africa they truly come from. That disconnect can impact **self-esteem** and **direction**.

Mini-Lesson Key Points (Middle School Level):

- Africa is a **continent**, not a country. It has **54 different countries** with different cultures and languages.

- Many of us were disconnected from our specific African roots during slavery, which is why our identity is often described in **vague, general terms**.
- We often use labels without really knowing the **history or meaning** behind them.
- The Bible can be read as a **historical text** as well as a spiritual one. (Genesis 6–10, Genesis 42:6–8, Exodus 2:19, Deuteronomy 28, Revelation 1:14–15) are examples you can reference to show our presence in Scripture.

Key Discussion Questions (Whole Group or Think-Pair-Share):

1. Does being called "African American" tell you exactly where your people come from? Why or why not?
2. How can not knowing your true origin affect how you feel about yourself?
3. Who usually gets to decide what we are called—us or other people?

Encourage students to use sentence stems like:

- "I used to think…, but now I'm starting to think…"
- "When people call me ___, it makes me feel…"

Activity – "Beyond the Label" Identity Reflection:

Students write a short response titled **"Who Am I Beyond a Label?"**
Guide them with prompts:

- What do I believe about myself?
- What do I want people to know about my history and my future?
- What makes me more than just a color or a word?

Students should write at least **one solid paragraph** (middle school appropriate, 6–8 sentences).

Real World Connection:
Share with students how schools often separate **history** from **faith** or spirituality (separation of church and state), which can cause important parts of our story to be left out. Explain that **miseducation** happens when pieces of the truth are removed.

Connect this idea to how media, textbooks, and even social media can shape how Black children see themselves.

Reflection Journal (Independent Writing):

Prompt:

What part of today's conversation made you rethink your own identity? Why?

Students write **two paragraphs**, using at least one of these starters:

- "I never realized that…"
- "Now I see that…"
- "This matters to me because…"

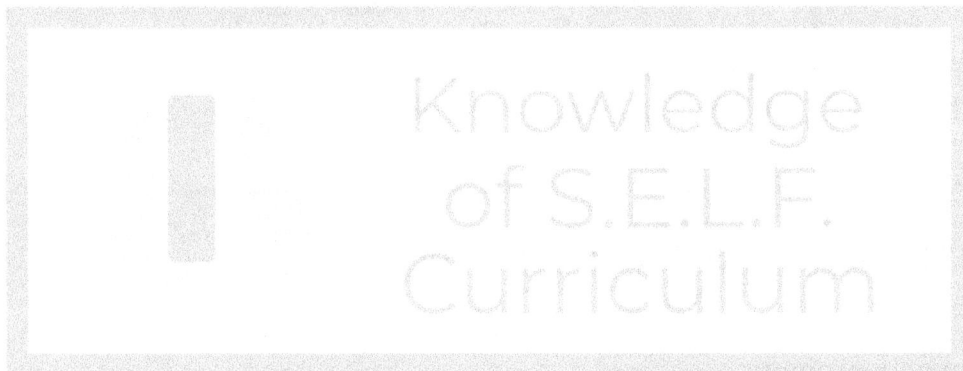

Lesson 2: Am I a Color? (Part 2)

Objective:
Students will continue building identity awareness by examining the words *Black* and *White* and connecting biblical history to their understanding of who they are.

Do Now (Student Prompt):
What is the purpose of going to church? What is the purpose of going to school?
List **two things** both have in common. (For example: learning, guidance, community, correction.)

Facilitator's Talk:
Explain that the Bible can be studied as **history**, not just religion. Revisit Deuteronomy 28 and the prophecy about a people experiencing **400 years of oppression**. Connect this to the Trans-Atlantic Slave Trade and how millions of Africans were taken from their land.

Make it middle-school clear:

- Slavery is **not** where our story begins.
- Our people had kingdoms, languages, science, math, and faith **before** slavery.
- When those truths are removed from school, our history looks like it starts in chains.

Stress that miseducation is **on purpose**, not by accident.

Mini-Lesson Key Points:

- The Trans-Atlantic Slave Trade disconnected millions from their languages, names, and specific African nations.
- Terms like *Black* and *White* became **social categories** used to justify who had power and who didn't.
- There is power in reconnecting to ancient history that shows us as **builders, leaders, and creators**, not just slaves.

Key Discussion Questions:

1. Why is it powerful for African American students to reconnect to ancient African and biblical history?
2. How might our schools and communities change if everybody knew the full truth?
3. What happens to a people when they are only taught their pain and not their greatness?

Activity – Scripture & History Connection:

Have students read a selected portion of **Deuteronomy 28** (you choose an age-appropriate section).
Then ask them to write a short response:

- What is happening in this passage?
- Do you see any connection between this and what you've learned about slavery in America?
- How does this make you feel about your identity and your people?

Encourage them to underline or highlight words that stand out (curse, scattered, strangers, etc.) and put those in their response.

Real World Connection:

Show a brief, age-appropriate clip from a documentary or animated explainer on the **Trans-Atlantic Slave Trade**.
Afterward, discuss:

- What did you see that you never knew before?
- How does that connect to Deuteronomy 28 or other scriptures you've seen?

Reflection Journal:

Prompt:

How would education change if true African and biblical history was taught from the beginning, not from slavery?

Students write **two paragraphs**, focusing on:

- How school might feel different
- How Black students might walk, talk, and dream differently

Lesson 3: Love Yourself — The Skin You're In

Objective: Teach students about melanin, instill self-love, and encourage pride in their natural identity.

Vocabulary Focus:
- Melanin: The pigment responsible for the color of skin, hair, and eyes.

Do Now:
Prompt: "Have you ever heard someone say, 'I don't want to get too dark'? What does that statement mean to you?"
Use this as a launch point for discussing internalized bias.

Mini-Lesson Delivery Tips:
• Explain melanin using the scientific breakdown: 6 protons, 6 neutrons, 6 electrons = 666.
• Deconstruct myths or fears around dark skin.
• Use a Skin Tone Chart to celebrate the full range of beauty among Black and Brown youth.

"I don't want to be in the sun too long because I don't want to get black." How many times have we either heard or said this comment? The very thing that we don't want to get is the sole source of our dominance, melanin. Melanin is made up of 6 protons, 6 neutrons, and 6 electrons, 666. When the numbers 666 are often mentioned it's referred by mainstream media as the mark of the beast.

However, when you gain knowledge of SELF, one begins to learn that the so called African American or black people aren't even the color that they sing loud and proud about. Look at the Skin Tone Chart and match your skin complexion with the shades of brown on the Skin Tone Chart.

<u>Critical Thinking time</u>: We talk about the power of words, so let's discuss the two terms we

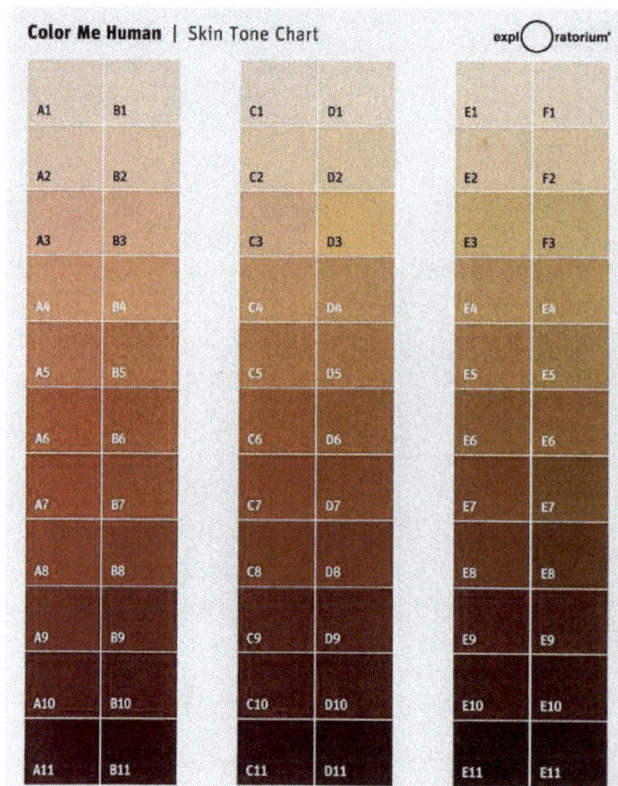

Color Me Human | Skin Tone Chart   expl◯ratorium'

A1	B1	C1	D1	E1	F1
A2	B2	C2	D2	E2	F2
A3	B3	C3	D3	E3	F3
A4	B4	C4	D4	E4	E4
A5	B5	C5	D5	E5	E5
A6	B6	C6	D6	E6	E6
A7	B7	C7	D7	E7	E7
A8	B8	C8	D8	E8	E8
A9	B9	C9	D9	E9	E9
A10	B10	C10	D10	E10	E10
A11	B11	C11	D11	E11	E11

use to describe people, black and white.

Have students go to Merriam Webster to define the terms black and white. Discuss with students the difference of the two terms and why if we say there are power in words, why do we identify ourselves with such a negative word? Why is the term white described positive? How do you feel about the information you learned today? Do you feel empowered?

Critical Thinking Discussion Guidance:
1. "How does understanding melanin empower your identity?"
2. "Why does the language we use matter when describing ourselves or others?"

Activity – Skin Tone Matching:
Distribute a skin tone chart or shade cards. Have students match their complexion and write how it feels to embrace their hue.

Reflection Journal:
Prompt: "How will you celebrate your true self starting today?" Encourage creativity, affirmations, and personal commitments.

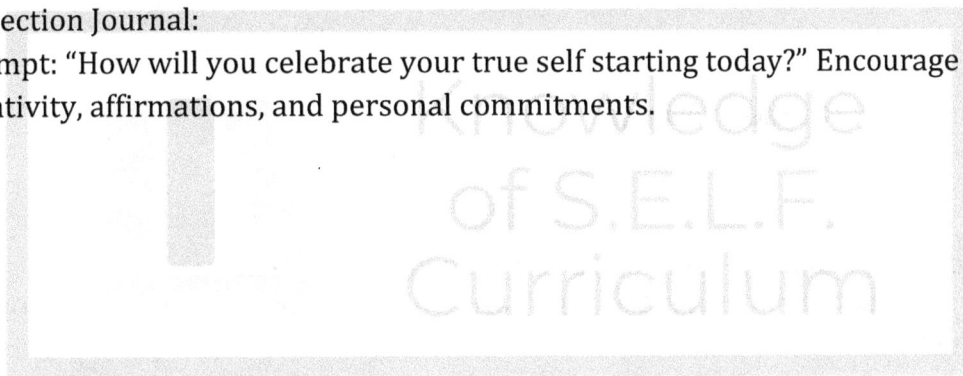

Lesson 4: Attributes/Characteristics of SELF

Objective:

Students will identify the qualities, traits, and characteristics that shape who they are while learning how those attributes influence their decisions, relationships, and future purpose.

Do Now (Student Prompt):

List **three positive qualities** you believe you have.
Examples: kind, focused, funny, brave, respectful, hardworking, creative.

Then answer:
Which of the three best represents who you are right now? Why?

Facilitator's Talk (Guided Script):

Say to the students:

"The world will try to name you before you even know yourself.
Today, we reclaim the narrative. You will learn who you ARE — not who the world told you to be."

Explain in middle-school clarity:

- **Attributes** are the parts of your personality that show who you are.
- Some attributes are natural — your personality, your vibe, the way you think.
- Some attributes are developed — your integrity, your leadership, your discipline.

Tell them:

"When you know your attributes, you don't have to copy anybody.
You walk different. You talk different. You choose different.
You move with purpose, not pressure."

Connect this to SELF Conscience:

- Knowing yourself helps you make better decisions.
- Knowing your strengths helps you lead instead of follow.

- Knowing your character helps you protect your future.

Mini-Lesson Key Points (Make an Anchor Chart):

1. **Attributes = The traits that define how you act and respond**
2. **Attributes influence your relationships and reputation**
3. **Your attributes can grow and evolve over time**
4. **Positive attributes strengthen your destiny**
5. **Awareness of SELF leads to better choices**

Use examples they recognize:

- A student who is honest builds trust.
- A hardworking student improves steadily.
- A patient student avoids drama.
- A focused student reaches goals faster.

Let them understand that attributes can be strengthened like muscles.

Guiding Questions (Whole Class or Groups):

1. Why is it important to know your own attributes?
2. Which attribute do you think is your strongest? How does it show up in your life?
3. Which attribute do you want to grow, and why?
4. How do your attributes affect the people around you? Your family? Your friends?

Encourage them to explore how traits influence decisions.

Activity — "I Am, I Can, I Will" Character Map

Students create a **character map** in three sections:

1. **I AM...**
   (5 attributes they believe describe who they are)
2. **I CAN...**
   (5 things they are capable of doing because of those attributes)
3. **I WILL...**
   (3 commitments they will make to grow their best qualities)

Example:

- I am: patient.
- I can: stay calm when things go wrong.
- I will: practice pausing before I react.

This helps students connect attributes → actions → plans.

Real World Connection:

Explain that people who change the world often share similar character traits:

- Discipline
- Courage
- Consistency
- Compassion
- Confidence
- Resilience

Share examples like:

- Athletes who train even when they're tired.
- Artists who practice every day before anyone knows their name.
- Community leaders who serve even when nobody claps.

Say:

"Your attributes will take you places talent can't.
People follow character before they follow skills."

Reflection Journal (Independent Writing):

Prompt:
Which personal attribute do you believe will help you shape your future the most? Explain how and why.

Students write **two paragraphs**:

- Paragraph 1: Explain the attribute
- Paragraph 2: Connect it to their goals, dreams, or relationships

---

Exit Ticket:

Circle one word:
Growth — Leadership — Consistency — Confidence — Courage

Write one sentence explaining why you chose it.

Lesson 5: Ethics

Objcctive:

Students will define ethics, identify their core values, and understand how personal ethics influence decisions, relationships, and leadership.

Do Now (Student Prompt):

List **three values** that matter to you:
Examples: honesty, loyalty, responsibility, fairness, courage, respect, self-control.

Then answer:
Which value do you struggle with the most and why?
(Be honest — no judgment.)

™

Facilitator's Talk (Guided Script):

Say to students:

"Every day, somebody is watching you — even when you don't notice.
Not to judge you... but to learn who you are."

Explain ethics in simple, middle-school clarity:

- **Ethics** are the personal rules you choose to live by.
- Ethics show what type of person you are **when nobody is watching**.
- Ethics help you stay grounded when pressure tries to pull you out of character.

Tell them:

"Your ethics are your GPS.
They guide your steps when your feelings get loud,
when friends get messy,
and when temptation gets real."

Make it real to them:

- Ethics help you say "no" to things that don't match your value system.
- Ethics help you choose peace over drama.

- Ethics help you stand firm even when others fall apart.

Mini-Lesson Key Points (Anchor Chart):

1. **Ethics = Personal standards + actions**
2. **Your values shape your decisions**
3. **Strong ethics protect your future**
4. **Ethics require consistency**
5. **Your reputation is built on your ethics**

Use middle-school examples:

- Not cheating even when the answer is right there
- Not laughing when a classmate gets bullied
- Telling the truth even when it's uncomfortable
- Walking away from drama because you know better
- Admitting mistakes without making excuses

Explain that ethics build trust — with others and with yourself.

Guiding Questions (Whole Class or Small Group):

1. Why is it important for young people to have strong ethics?
2. Which value do you believe needs to be stronger in your life right now?
3. How can your ethics help you stay out of drama or trouble?
4. What happens when someone's actions don't match their values?

Encourage honesty, introspection, and real talk.

Activity — My Ethics Code Statement

Students write a short **Ethics Statement** using these sentence starters:

- "I believe in..."
- "I will not..."
- "I will work on..."
- "When I feel pressured, I will remember..."
- "I choose to be a person who..."

Model one for them:

"I believe in honesty.
I will not allow friends to pressure me into doing wrong.
When I feel tempted, I will remember who I'm becoming   not where I've been.
I choose to be a person who leads with integrity."

Students write **one full paragraph (5–7 sentences)**.

Real World Connection:

Explain that ethics matter everywhere:

- At school
- At home
- On a team
- In relationships
- On social media
- In future careers

Give real-life scenarios:

- A student finds money on the floor — do they keep it or return it?
- Someone gets blamed for something you saw — do you speak up?
- A group is making fun of someone — do you join in or shut it down?

Tell them:

"Your ethics are your armor.
They protect you from becoming the person you never wanted to be."

Reflection Journal:

Prompt:
Write about a time when you had to choose between doing what was easy and doing what was right. What did you learn from that moment?

Students write **two paragraphs**:

- Paragraph 1: Describe the moment
- Paragraph 2: Reflect on the lesson

Exit Ticket:

Complete the sentence:
"My ethics matter because they help me _____."

Lesson 6: Image

Objective:

Students will understand the difference between the image they project and the truth of who they really are, learning how authenticity builds confidence, trust, and healthy identity.

Do Now (Student Prompt):

In one word, describe how you *want* people to see you.
Examples: confident, real, kind, smart, loyal, brave.

Then answer:
Is this how you actually show up every day? Why or why not?

Facilitator's Talk (Guided Script):

Say to the students:

"We live in a world where everybody wants to be seen — but very few want to be known."

Explain in middle-school clarity:

- **Image** = What people think about you based on what they see
- **Identity** = Who you really are on the inside

Tell them:

"Your image can be edited.
Your identity cannot."

Break it down:

- Social media can make you look confident when you're actually insecure.
- A smile can hide sadness.
- A tough attitude can hide fear.
- Popularity can hide loneliness.
- "Acting grown" can hide confusion.

Then say:

"I don't want the world to meet your filtered self.
I want the world to meet **you** — the version God created on purpose."

Mini-Lesson Key Points (Anchor Chart):

1. **Image = The mask**
2. **Identity = The truth**
3. **Authenticity builds stronger relationships than performance**
4. **Social media is not your teacher**
5. **When your image and identity match, you walk in peace**

Give relatable examples:

- Posting a happy picture after crying
- Acting like you don't care when you really do
- Pretending to be tough to avoid being picked on
- Dressing a certain way to fit in
- Changing your personality depending on who you're with

Let them see themselves without judgment — only truth.

Guiding Questions (Whole Group or Pair Share):

1. Why do you think kids your age feel pressure to create a certain image?
2. What's the danger of pretending to be someone you're not?
3. How does being authentic help you make better friends?
4. What do you think your image says about you right now?

Encourage vulnerability but protect emotional safety.

Activity — "My Two Selves" Reflection

Students draw two boxes:

Box 1: "The Me People See"
They write 4–5 qualities or behaviors others recognize (examples: quiet, funny, athletic, shy, loud, serious).

Box 2: "The Real Me"
They write 4–5 qualities they feel internally (examples: caring, stressed, confident, confused, hopeful, frustrated).

Then ask:

- What is the difference between the two?
- Which box feels more authentic?
- What needs to change so your image matches your true self?

Guide gently — this activity often reveals deep insight.

Real World Connection:

Explain that celebrities, influencers, and even adults struggle with image:

- Some pretend to be perfect.
- Some hide mistakes to avoid embarrassment.
- Some pretend to be confident because they fear judgment.

Tell students:

"The strongest version of you is the honest one.
Pretending is exhausting.
Authenticity is freedom."

Share examples of public figures who are known for their authenticity — people respected not for perfection, but for honesty and consistency.

Reflection Journal:

Prompt:
What is one part of yourself you want the world to see more clearly? Why is that important to you?

Students write **two paragraphs**:

- Paragraph 1: Describe the trait/quality
- Paragraph 2: Explain why revealing it will help them grow

Exit Ticket:

Complete the sentence:
"I am choosing authenticity over image because..."

Lesson 7: Achievements

Objective:

Students will identify their personal achievements—big or small—and learn how celebrating progress builds confidence, discipline, and a stronger sense of SELF.

Do Now (Student Prompt):

Think about this school year so far.
Write down one thing you accomplished that makes you proud.

It can be academic, athletic, emotional, behavioral, artistic, or personal.

Then answer:
How did that achievement make you feel?

Facilitator's Talk (Guided Script):

Say to the students:

"Some of your greatest achievements aren't trophies — they're the battles nobody else saw you win."

Break it down in middle-school clarity:

- Waking up every day when you felt overwhelmed is an achievement.
- Raising your grades is an achievement.
- Choosing not to fight back is an achievement.
- Apologizing when you were wrong is an achievement.
- Becoming more responsible is an achievement.
- Staying focused when distractions were loud is an achievement.

Tell them:

"You have survived things that would have broken other people your age.
But you're still here — learning, growing, and pushing."

Explain how society often celebrates the wrong things:

- Followers

- Popularity
- Trends
- Drama
- Image

But in **SELF Conscience**, we celebrate:

- Growth
- Discipline
- Courage
- Emotional maturity
- Kindness
- Resilience
- Character

Mini-Lesson Key Points (Anchor Chart):

1. **Achievements show your growth and progress**
2. **Small wins lead to big wins**
3. **Celebrating your achievements builds confidence**
4. **Achievements strengthen your identity and self-trust**
5. **Your achievements are the foundation of your future goals**

Give relatable examples:

- Turning in assignments on time
- Improving behavior in class
- Helping siblings at home
- Being a better friend
- Setting boundaries
- Being consistent in something new

Let them see how their everyday efforts matter.

Guiding Questions (Whole Group or Small Group):

1. Why is it important to recognize your own achievements?
2. How can celebrating small wins help you reach bigger goals?
3. What achievement this year surprised you the most?
4. What achievement are you still working toward right now?

Encourage sharing — this builds community and peer affirmation.

Activity — "Victory Log" (Signature Activity)

Students create a **Victory Log** page.

Part 1: List 5 Achievements
These can be from school, home, sports, friendships, mindset changes, etc.

Part 2: For each achievement, write:

- **What happened?**
- **What did this teach me about myself?**
- **Why does this achievement matter?**

Part 3: Circle the achievement that changed you the most.

This builds reflection, pride, and SEL awareness.

Real World Connection:

Explain that every successful person you know began with *small wins*:

- An athlete practiced early before anyone noticed.
- An artist drew for years before someone praised them.
- A leader made better decisions long before they led others.
- A musician practiced scales before performing songs.

Say:

"Every win is a brick.
Every lesson is a brick.
Every achievement — small or big — builds the future you're stepping into."

Connect it back to SELF:

- Achievements help you believe in yourself.
- Achievements teach discipline.
- Achievements are proof that you're capable of more.

Reflection Journal:

Prompt:
Which achievement are you most proud of, and how does it reflect the person you are becoming?

Students write **two paragraphs**:

- Paragraph 1: Describe the achievement
- Paragraph 2: Connect it to their identity and future goals

Exit Ticket:

Complete the sentence:
"My next achievement will be _____ because I'm ready to _____."

Knowledge of SELF Middle School Facilitator's Guide

Unit 2: SELF GOVERNING

Lesson 1: Health & Nutrition

Objective:

Students will understand how taking care of their physical body strengthens their mind, discipline, focus, behavior, and future power.

Do Now (Student Prompt):

Write down everything you ate in the last 24 hours.
Then answer:
Did the food you ate give you energy... or take energy away?

Facilitator's Talk (Guided Script):

Tell students:

"Your body is the first classroom you ever had.
If the body shuts down, the mind can't focus.
If the body is weak, the emotions become unstable.
If the body is unhealthy, the spirit loses clarity."

Teach them:

- Food is **fuel**, not filler.
- What you eat can help you focus... or distract you.
- Good health is not about being skinny or muscular — it's about **discipline**.
- Healthy habits = long life, clarity, self-control, strength.

Share examples:

- Eating too much sugar → brain fog, mood swings
- Skipping meals → irritability, headaches
- Drinking water → better skin, better focus, better energy
- Sleeping enough → better decision making

Make it relevant:

"Some of us aren't 'bad kids.' We're just tired, dehydrated, and underfed."

Mini-Lesson Key Points (Anchor Chart):

1. **Nutrition affects emotions and behavior**
2. **Healthy choices improve focus and memory**
3. **Sleep is a superpower — not an option**
4. **Water heals more than you think**
5. **Your health is your responsibility, not someone else's**

Guiding Questions:

1. How does what you eat affect your mood and focus?
2. What unhealthy habits do you want to change?
3. Why do you think young people struggle with routines like sleep, water, hygiene, and meals?
4. How can taking care of your body help you avoid drama?

Activity — "Build a Better Day"

Students create a **healthy daily routine plan**, including:

- Wake-up time
- Breakfast choice
- Water goals
- Snack choices
- Movement/exercise
- Bedtime
- Screen limits

Make them write one **non-negotiable** healthy change they will begin this week.

Real World Connection:

Explain:

- Most leaders wake up early.
- Athletes eat for performance, not cravings.
- Entrepreneurs follow routines.
- Greatness requires consistency.

Tell them:

"If you want to separate yourself from average, start with your discipline — not your social media."

Reflection Journal:

What is one new healthy habit you want to build, and how will it help your future self?

Exit Ticket:

Complete the sentence:
"Starting today, my health matters because…"

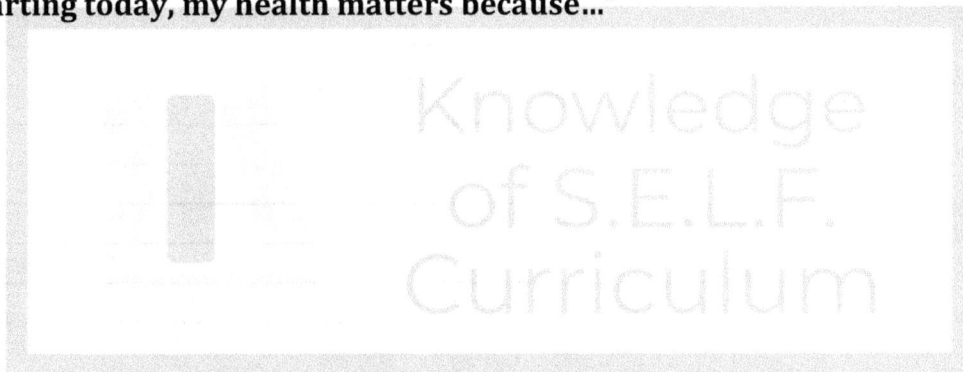

Lesson 2: The Importance of FOCUS

Objective:
Students will learn how to cultivate FOCUS using the Knowledge of SELF framework:
Fallback, Opportunities, Cultivate, Understanding, Succeed.

Do Now:
Describe a time when you struggled to stay focused. What distracted you?

_____

_____

_____

_____

_____

_____

_____

_____

_____

_____

_____

_____

_____

_____

Facilitator's Talk:
Explain Cedric A. Washington's method of FOCUS:
- Fallback: Remove distractions.
- Opportunities: Align yourself with positive environments and mentors.
- Cultivate: Practice and refine your craft.
- Understanding: Accept that everyone won't understand your vision.
- Succeed: Celebrate the milestones along the way.

Mini-Lesson Key Points:
- FOCUS is not natural — it's developed.
- FOCUS leads to vision and vision leads to destiny.

Key Discussion Questions:
1. How can falling back from your comfort zone sharpen your focus?
2. How does understanding the misunderstanding of others empower you?

Activity:

FOCUS Action Plan — Students create personal FOCUS blueprints using the method taught.

Real World Connection:

Watch Cedric A. Washington's TEDx Talk on Focus 'How to use FOCUS to become a Trailblazer' and reflect on key takeaways.

Reflection Journal:

What step of FOCUS will you strengthen most this month?
[Write two full paragraphs.]

_____

_____

_____

_____

_____

_____

_____

_____

_____

_____

_____

_____

_____

_____

_____

_____

_____

_____

_____

_____

_____

_____

_____

_____

_____

_____

_____

Lesson 3: Role Modeling

Objective:

Students will learn what it means to be a role model and how their actions influence others whether they realize it or not.

Do Now:

Who do you look up to?
(List one person and why you admire them.)

Facilitator's Talk:

Tell them:

"You are a role model — whether you signed up for it or not."

Explain:

- Younger kids watch them.
- Classmates study their behavior.
- Family members mimic their moods.
- Someone is learning from them every day.

Teach:

"A role model isn't someone perfect.
It's someone consistent."

Mini-Lesson Key Points:

1. **You influence someone daily**
2. **Leadership is shown through behavior, not popularity**
3. **Being a role model means being responsible for your impact**
4. **People follow courage, compassion, and consistency**
5. **Your character teaches louder than your voice**

Guiding Questions:

1. What traits make a strong role model?
2. How can you be a positive example without being "perfect"?
3. What's one thing you do that younger students might copy?
4. Why does being a role model matter?

Activity — "My Influence Map"

Students write:

- People who influence them (family, peers, teachers, celebrities)
- People they influence (siblings, friends, classmates)
- One behavior they will improve because others are watching

Real World Connection:

Explain how communities rise and fall based on leadership examples:

- Negative leaders create chaos
- Positive leaders create culture
- Young leaders inspire hope

Tell them:

"If you want a better community, start by becoming a better YOU."

Reflection Journal:

What kind of role model are you right now, and what kind do you want to become? Explain.

Exit Ticket:

Complete:
"A leader is someone who _____."

Lesson 4: Hygiene

Objectives

Students will understand how personal hygiene impacts confidence, social interactions, self-respect, and emotional well-being.

Do Now:

Why does hygiene matter?
(Write 2–3 sentences.)

Facilitator's Talk:

Say:

"Hygiene is not about being 'fancy' — it's about respect. Respect for yourself and others."

Explain:

- Cleanliness affects how peers treat you
- Clean clothes change your mood
- Brushing teeth affects self-confidence and health
- Body odor is preventable and fixable
- Hygiene is part of **self-governing**, not embarrassment

Let them know:

"Taking care of your body is a sign of emotional maturity."

Mini-Lesson Key Points:

1. **Hygiene affects confidence**
2. **Cleanliness impacts how people perceive you**
3. **Poor hygiene can cause illness**
4. **Scent and appearance influence social interactions**
5. **Healthy routines build strong discipline**

Guiding Questions:

1. How does good hygiene help you feel more confident?
2. Why do some students struggle with hygiene?
3. How can you improve your daily routine?
4. What is one hygiene habit you need to strengthen?

Activity — "Daily Reset Routine"

Students create a checklist including:

- Shower/bath
- Brushing teeth
- Deodorant
- Clean clothes
- Lotion
- Hair care
- Fresh mask/face covering if applicable
- Night routine

They must write **why each step matters**.

Real World Connection:

Teach:

- Employers judge hygiene
- Coaches require hygiene for teams
- Poor hygiene affects friendships
- Confidence grows when you feel clean and prepared

Say:

"People treat you like you treat yourself.
Show the world your best you."

Reflection Journal:

Which hygiene habit is most important for you to improve, and how will you start today?

_____

Exit Ticket:

One sentence:
"My hygiene shows _____."

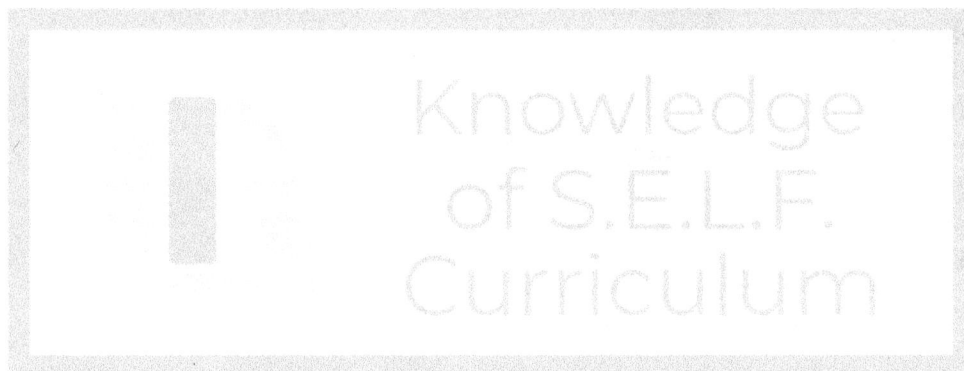

Lesson 5: Emotional Maturity

Objective:

Students will recognize signs of emotional maturity and learn how to manage feelings in healthy, responsible ways.

Do Now:

What do you do when you feel angry or frustrated?
Be honest and list 2–3 behaviors.

Facilitator's Talk:

Say:

"Growing up is not about size — it's about emotional control."

Teach:

- Emotional maturity = managing your reactions
- Acting on impulse leads to regret
- Thinking before reacting is a sign of strength
- Not every emotion deserves a response

Tell them:

"You don't lose control — you give it away."

Mini-Lesson Key Points:

1. **Feelings are real, but they are not facts**
2. **Maturity = pause + think + choose**
3. **You are responsible for your reactions**
4. **Emotional maturity makes life easier**
5. **Growth requires self-control**

Guiding Questions:

1. What situation usually makes you lose control?
2. Why is it important to respond instead of react?
3. How can emotional maturity help you at school?
4. What does an emotionally mature person look like?

Activity — "Reaction vs. Response" Chart

Students list common triggers:

- Someone insults you
- A teacher corrects you
- You feel embarrassed
- A friend betrays you
- Someone spreads rumors

Then they write:
How I used to react vs. **How I want to respond now**

Real World Connection:

Explain:

- Adults lose jobs because they can't control emotions
- Teens get suspended because they react too fast
- Relationships break because people can't communicate
- Leaders rise because they remain calm

Tell them:

"Control your emotions or your emotions will control you."

Reflection Journal:

Describe a moment when emotional maturity could have changed the outcome of a situation. What would you do differently today?

Exit Ticket:

Complete:
"Emotional maturity helps me _____."

Lesson 6: Puberty

Objective:

Students will understand the physical, emotional, and social changes of puberty and learn how to navigate them respectfully and confidently.

Do Now:

What is one question you have about growing up?
(Anonymous option recommended.)

Facilitator's Talk:

Say:

"Puberty is not something to fear or be embarrassed about — it's the process of becoming who you were designed to be."

Explain the changes:

- Body odor
- Growth spurts
- Hormones
- Voice changes
- Breasts developing
- Facial/body hair
- Emotional shifts
- Mood swings
- Attraction and curiosity

Normalize everything:

"Nothing about puberty is weird.
What's weird is pretending it isn't happening."

Teach:

- Respect for self

- Respect for others
- Privacy
- Boundaries
- Hygiene
- Emotional understanding

Mini-Lesson Key Points:

1. **Everyone develops differently**
2. **Puberty is a sign of growth, not shame**
3. **Feelings become stronger — control becomes more important**
4. **Boundaries keep relationships healthy**
5. **Hygiene becomes critical during adolescence**

Guiding Questions:

1. Why do you think puberty makes some students insecure?
2. How can knowing what to expect make the process easier?
3. Why is respect important during this stage of life?
4. What advice would you give someone struggling with these changes?

Activity — "Growing With Grace" Worksheet

Students write:

- 3 changes they've noticed
- 2 questions they have
- 2 positive affirmations ("I am growing." "I am normal.")
- 1 healthy habit they will add during this stage

Real World Connection:

Explain:

- Every adult they admire experienced puberty
- How they handle this stage influences confidence, friendships, and behavior
- Early emotional maturity prevents bad decisions later

Tell them:

"This is not the time to copy the world — it's the time to build your foundation."

Reflection Journal:

What is one change you're experiencing or expecting, and how can you handle it with maturity?

Exit Ticket:

Fill in:
"I will handle puberty with maturity by _____."

Lesson 7: Peer Pressure

Objective:

Students will recognize different forms of peer pressure, understand how it influences behavior, and learn skills to resist unhealthy influence.

Do Now:

Write down a time when someone tried to influence you to do something you did **not** want to do.

Facilitator's Talk:

Say:

"Pressure is real. But identity is stronger than influence."

Teach:

- Peer pressure can be direct or indirect
- It can be verbal, emotional, or silent
- You can be pressured into behavior or pressured out of dreams
- Knowing yourself protects you from manipulation

Tell them:

"If you don't stand for something, you'll fall for anything."

Mini-Lesson Key Points:

1. **Peer pressure isn't always loud — it can be subtle**
2. **Your choices shape your reputation and future**
3. **Friends who pressure you aren't friends**
4. **Saying NO is a skill, not an attitude**
5. **You protect your destiny by protecting your environment**

Guiding Questions:

1. Why do you think people pressure others?
2. What makes saying "no" difficult?
3. How does peer pressure affect behavior and grades?
4. What kind of people should you surround yourself with?

Activity — "Power Lines" Practice

Students practice saying:

- "Nah, I'm good."
- "That's not me."
- "I'm not risking my future."
- "If you're my friend, don't pressure me."

They write:

- 3 unhealthy pressures they face
- 3 responses they can use
- 1 safe adult they can talk to

Real World Connection:

Explain:

- Teens lose opportunities because of one pressured decision
- School fights, vaping, sex, violence, skipping class often start with pressure
- Leaders choose environments that match their purpose

Tell them:

"Your circle either pushes you forward or pulls you down.
Make the choice — don't let the choice make you."

Reflection Journal:

What is one type of peer pressure you want to overcome, and how will you respond next time?

Exit Ticket:

Complete:
"Peer pressure will not control me because I know my _____."

Knowledge of SELF Middle School Facilitator's Guide

Unit 3: SOCIAL CONSCIENCE™

Lesson 1: How to Be Effective in Your Community

Objective:

Students will understand what "community" truly means and identify practical ways they can make positive impact right now — not when they're older, not when they're "ready," but today.

Do Now (Student Prompt):

What is one problem in your community, neighborhood, or school that you wish you could fix?

Write **3 sentences** explaining why it matters to you.

Facilitator's Talk (Guided Script):

Say:

"Your community is not just where you live — it's who you are responsible for."

Explain that *community* includes:

- School
- Home
- Neighborhood
- Friends
- Teams
- Online spaces

Teach them:

- Every community either lifts people up or pulls people down.
- Every person — even a middle school student — has power to influence their environment.
- Leadership is not age-dependent; it's purpose-dependent.

Tell them:

"You don't need money to make impact.
You need awareness, compassion, and action."

Mini-Lesson Key Points (Anchor Chart):

1. **Community = People you grow with**
2. **Your voice matters**
3. **Small actions create big change**
4. **Leaders solve problems, not just talk about them**
5. **Every strong community has young leaders holding it together**

Examples:

- Cleaning up trash
- Standing up for bullied kids
- Helping a classmate understand work
- Being positive on your block
- Supporting younger siblings
- Choosing peace instead of drama

Guiding Questions:

1. What makes a community strong?
2. What community work can students your age actually do?
3. Why do some people complain about problems but never try to fix them?
4. What is one strength you have that could help others?

Activity — "Change Starts With Me" Action Sheet

Students identify:

- **1 problem** they see
- **1 cause** of the problem
- **1 solution** they can help with
- **1 step** they will take this week

Example:

- Problem: Kids getting bullied
- Cause: Peer pressure, insecurity
- Solution: Create safe spaces, speak up
- Action: Check on isolated students, refuse to laugh at bullying

---

Real World Connection:

Explain that major leaders began young:

- Dr. King was influenced by youth leaders
- Civil Rights marches included children
- Movements like Black Lives Matter included teens
- Community change often starts with the youngest voices

Tell them:

"If you want a stronger community, be the seed.
Growth starts with you."

Reflection Journal:

**What positive change do you want to be known for in your community?
Why is that important to you?**

Exit Ticket:

Finish:
"I can impact my community by _____."

Lesson 2: African American Leaders

Objective:

Students will learn about influential African American leaders historically and locally, understanding that leadership is not limited to famous names — leadership is built, grown, and lived every day.

Do Now:

Name **one African American leader** you admire.
Write one sentence explaining why.

Facilitator's Talk:

Say:

"Before your favorite celebrity, before your favorite influencer — there were leaders who carried weight, legacy, and vision."

Teach:

- Leadership isn't driven by fame; it's driven by impact.
- Some of our greatest leaders weren't loud — they were disciplined.
- You don't have to wait until you're grown to lead.

Give them examples beyond the basic school textbook list:

- **Ella Baker** – Power in community organizing
- **Fred Hampton** – Leadership rooted in unity
- **Fannie Lou Hamer** – Courage and truth-telling
- **Benjamin E. Mays** – Academic excellence
- **Shirley Chisholm** – Breaking barriers
- **Septima Clark** – Education activism

Explain:

"Leaders don't just change history — they change neighborhoods.
They change classrooms.
They change families."

Mini-Lesson Key Points:

1. **Leadership begins with responsibility**
2. **Black history is full of world-changing youth**
3. **You are part of a legacy of excellence**
4. **Leadership requires courage and conviction**
5. **Your leadership will outlive your lifetime**

Guiding Questions:

1. What makes a leader worth following?
2. How do young people change the world?
3. What leadership qualities do YOU have?
4. Why is representation important?

Activity — "Leader Spotlight" Creation

Students choose one African American leader and create a **Leadership Spotlight** including:

- Photo (optional)
- Major contributions
- Character traits
- One lesson they teach YOU

Students present or share in groups.

Real World Connection:

Tell students:

"Black leaders didn't wait for permission — they moved with purpose."

Remind them that leadership:

- Happens in school hallways
- Happens in homes
- Happens in friend groups

- Happens in silence
- Happens in choices

Reflection Journal:

Which leadership trait do you want to strengthen, and how will you begin?

Exit Ticket:

Complete:
"A leader I want to be like is _____ because _____."

Lesson 3: Hip Hop — The Culture

Objective:

Students will explore hip-hop as a cultural movement shaped by African American creativity, expression, struggle, and truth — learning to separate culture from harmful industry messaging.

Do Now:

Who is your favorite hip-hop artist or group?
Why?

Facilitator's Talk:

Say:

"Hip-hop is not just music — it's culture, creativity, resistance, and identity."

Teach them:

- Hip-hop was born in the Bronx (1970s) from struggle, joy, rhythm, and storytelling.
- It was a voice for the unheard.
- The four elements: MCing, DJing, Breakdancing, Graffiti Art.
- Hip-hop was originally about truth, pain, unity, and celebration.

Tell them:

"Hip-hop today is powerful — but parts of the industry push messages that don't match our values."

Explain:

- Culture = art, creativity, storytelling
- Industry = money, manipulation, stereotypes

Mini-Lesson Key Points:

1. **Hip-hop was created as empowerment**
2. **Lyrics reflect lived experiences**
3. **Not all hip-hop is positive or negative — it's diverse**
4. **Students must think critically about messages**
5. **Hip-hop is global Black influence**

Guiding Questions:

1. What messages do you hear in modern hip-hop?
2. How does hip-hop influence behavior and self-image?
3. How can hip-hop be used for change, not harm?
4. What is the difference between celebrating culture vs. glorifying destruction?

Activity — "Lyrics That Lift"

Students find (or are given) a verse with a **positive message**, then:

- Highlight key lines
- Identify the message
- Explain why it matters
- Connect it to their own life

Artists can include: J. Cole, Kendrick Lamar, Rapsody, Lauryn Hill, Common, Chance, etc.

Real World Connection:

Explain:

- Hip-hop influences fashion, language, politics, mental health, and social issues.
- Their generation consumes more music than any before.
- Hip-hop can either elevate them or distract them.

Tell them:

"Protect what you feed your spirit.
Not every vibe is for your future."

Reflection Journal:

How has hip-hop shaped you — positively or negatively? Be honest.

_____

Exit Ticket:

Complete:
"Hip-hop teaches me _____."

_____

_____

Lesson 4: Family Dynamics

Objective:

Students will understand how family influences identity, emotions, decisions, and future patterns — and learn how to grow positively even when family situations are difficult.

Do Now:

Describe one thing your family does well.
("Family" can include guardians, grandparents, siblings, foster family, etc.)

Facilitator's Talk:

Say:

"Every family has strengths.
Every family has struggles.
And every student carries both into the classroom."

Teach gently and respectfully:

- Families shape emotional habits
- Families teach communication patterns
- Families can pass down trauma *or* healing
- Students are not defined by family mistakes
- They can create new patterns and futures

Tell them:

"Your family is your foundation — but YOU are the architect of your future."

Mini-Lesson Key Points:

1. **Family affects identity deeply**
2. **Patterns can be repeated or broken**
3. **Home environment impacts school success**
4. **You can become the change your family needs**

5. **Love shows up in many forms**

Guiding Questions:

1. What is one strength in your family?
2. What is one challenge your family faces?
3. How do family patterns influence your behavior?
4. How can you be a positive change in your household?

Activity — "My Family Blueprint"

Students draw two columns:

Column A — Patterns I Want to Keep
Examples:

- Working hard
- Cooking together
- Humor
- Prayer
- Protecting each other

Column B — Patterns I Want to Break
Examples:

- Yelling
- Avoiding problems
- Giving up
- Being late
- Not communicating

Real World Connection:

Explain:

- Many successful people grew up in hard homes
- Their strength came from choosing different patterns
- Students can become cycle breakers

Tell them:

"You are not the problem — you are the solution your family has been waiting for."

Reflection Journal:

What is one new positive pattern you want to start in your family? Why?

Exit Ticket:

Complete:
"My family taught me _____."

Lesson 5: Accountability

Objective:

Students will understand the importance of taking responsibility for their actions and choices — without excuses, deflection, or blame.

Do Now:

Why is it hard to admit when you're wrong?
Be honest.

Facilitator's Talk:

Say:

"Accountability is not punishment — it's power."

Teach:

- Accountability = responsibility + honesty
- Excuses keep you stuck
- Growth requires ownership
- Blaming others blocks blessings

Tell them:

"You cannot fix what you refuse to face."

Break it down:

- When you own your actions, people trust you
- When you deflect, people stop believing you
- When you take responsibility, you gain respect

Mini-Lesson Key Points:

1. **Blaming is easy — owning is powerful**
2. **Accountability protects relationships**

3. **Leaders admit mistakes, then correct them**
4. **Growth requires uncomfortable truth**
5. **Accountability builds maturity**

Guiding Questions:

1. Why do people avoid accountability?
2. How does responsibility improve friendships?
3. What does a responsible student look like?
4. Why does accountability matter in adulthood?

Activity — "Own It, Fix It, Grow From It"

Students reflect on a moment where they:

- Made a mistake
- Hurt someone
- Broke a rule
- Avoided responsibility

They write:

- **What I did**
- **Why it happened**
- **What I should have done**
- **How I'll grow from it**

Real World Connection:

Explain:

- Jobs require accountability
- Relationships require accountability
- School success requires accountability
- Leadership requires accountability

Tell them:

"People don't expect perfection — they expect honesty."

Reflection Journal:

Write about a moment you took responsibility for something. How did it change the situation?

Exit Ticket:

Complete:
"I will be accountable by _____."

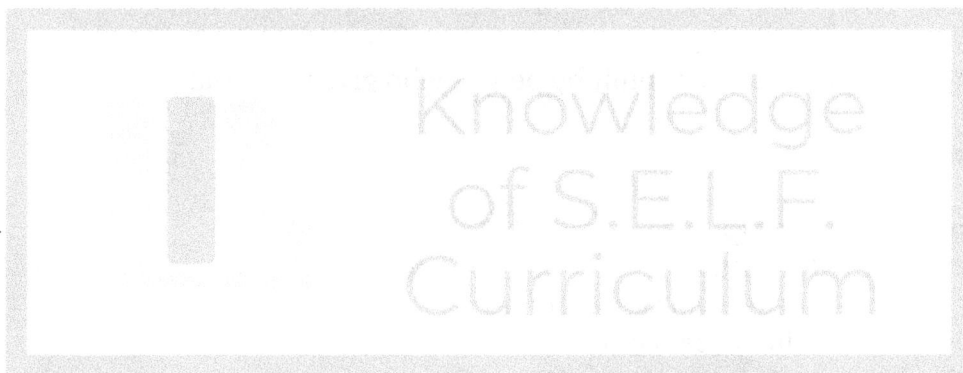

Lesson 6: Community Service & Giving Back

Objective:

Students will understand why service matters and how giving back builds character, leadership, empathy, and legacy.

Do Now:

Write one way someone has helped you this month.

Facilitator's Talk:

Say:

"The strongest communities are built by people who give more than they take."

Teach them:

- Service is leadership
- Service builds gratitude
- Service shifts focus from self → others
- Helping others increases confidence
- Giving back creates purpose

Tell them:

"When you lift others, you rise too."

Mini-Lesson Key Points:

1. **Service is a sign of maturity**
2. **Helping others strengthens empathy**
3. **Giving back builds character**
4. **Small acts matter**
5. **Service creates a sense of belonging**

Guiding Questions:

1. Why does giving back feel good?
2. How can students your age serve their community?
3. What stops people from helping others?
4. Who in your life needs support right now?

Activity — "Service Mission Plan"

Students choose **one service idea** they can complete within a week:

- Helping a younger sibling with homework
- Cleaning their block
- Writing a card to a teacher or relative
- Encouraging a classmate
- Organizing notebooks for someone
- Picking up trash
- Donating clothes

They write:

- What I will do
- Who it helps
- Why it matters

Real World Connection:

Share:

- Every great movement included service
- Leaders began with small acts
- Service builds humility and strength

Tell them:

"If you want to change the world, start with one person."

Reflection Journal:

Describe a moment when someone's kindness changed your day. How can you do that for someone else?

_____

Exit Ticket:

Complete:
"I can serve my community by _____."

_____

_____
_____

Lesson 7: Building Your Legacy

Objective:

Students will understand that legacy is created through daily choices and begin identifying how they want to be remembered.

Do Now:

What do you want people to say about you when you're not around?

Facilitator's Talk:

Say:

"Legacy is not built when you die — it is built while you live."

Teach:

- Legacy = the impact you leave behind
- Every action builds or breaks your legacy
- Legacies are built through character, not popularity

Tell them:

"Every day, you're writing the story people will remember."

Explain:

- Students can build legacy at home
- Students can build legacy at school
- Students can build legacy in peer groups
- Students can build legacy online
- Students can build legacy through goals and habits

Mini-Lesson Key Points:

1. **Legacy is built daily**
2. **Your decisions shape your reputation**

3. **What you repeat becomes who you are**
4. **You choose your impact**
5. **Legacy is leadership in motion**

Guiding Questions:

1. What kind of legacy do you want to leave?
2. How do your current habits influence your future?
3. What do you want younger kids to learn from you?
4. How will you build a legacy of excellence?

Activity — "Legacy Blueprint"

Students create a **three-part legacy plan**:

Part 1: Who I Want to Be
(Character traits, habits, values)

Part 2: What I Want to Leave Behind
(Memories, achievements, examples)

Part 3: How I Will Start Today
(Behavior changes, positive acts, daily habits)

Real World Connection:

Explain:

- Legacies are built by ordinary people doing extraordinary consistent things
- They inherit both positive and negative legacies
- They can break negative cycles and create new ones

Tell them:

"Your legacy begins the moment you decide to become intentional."

Reflection Journal:

What legacy do you want your future children, students, or community to remember you for? Why?

Exit Ticket:

Complete:
"My legacy will be _____."

Knowledge of SELF Middle School Facilitator's Guide

Unit 4: ASPIRATIONS

Knowledge of S.E.L.F. Curriculum

Lesson 1: What I Want to Be When I Grow Up

Objective:

Students will begin exploring career interests, personal gifts, and future possibilities while understanding that aspirations evolve as self-knowledge increases.

Do Now (Student Prompt):

Write down **three careers** you think you might want to pursue.
Then answer:
Why do these careers interest you?

Encourage honesty — no dream is too big or too small.

Facilitator's Talk (Guided Script):

Say:

"When you were born, you were born with purpose.
Not just personality. Not just potential.
Purpose."

Explain in middle-school clarity:

- Careers are not about money alone — they're about fulfillment.
- Students don't have to have everything figured out today.
- Their dreams may change, grow, or evolve as they learn more about themselves.
- What matters now is curiosity, exploration, and exposure.

Tell them:

"Stop asking, 'What job makes the most money?'
Start asking, 'What life was I created to live?'"

Explain:

- Careers connected to passion last longer.
- Careers connected to gifts create excellence.
- Careers connected to purpose create impact.

Mini-Lesson Key Points (Anchor Chart):

1. **Your dream is allowed to change**
2. **Internships, volunteering, and hobbies help you discover gifts**
3. **Your strengths point you toward purpose**
4. **Confidence grows when you imagine your future**
5. **Exposure expands possibilities**

Examples they'll understand:

- If you love helping people → social work, medicine, counseling, education
- If you love building things → engineering, architecture, construction, design
- If you love talking → law, sales, speaking, radio
- If you're creative → graphic design, music, digital production
- If you love fixing problems → IT, technology, entrepreneurship
- If you love justice → law, advocacy, public policy

Guiding Questions:

1. What are your natural gifts?
2. Which career matches your personality the most?
3. What job would you choose even if nobody clapped for you?
4. What future do you see when you close your eyes?

Activity — "Future Snapshot"

Students draw or write a **snapshot** of themselves at age 25:

- Career
- Location
- Lifestyle
- Values
- Relationship with family
- Personal goals
- Their impact on the world

Then students write a paragraph titled:
"A Day in My Life at Age 25."

This makes their future *tangible*.

Real World Connection:

Explain:

- Many people end up in jobs they don't love because they never explored their gifts early.
- Success comes from clarity + discipline + exposure.
- They don't need to wait until high school to dream big.

Tell them:

"The earlier you plan, the easier your life becomes."

Reflection Journal:

What career do you want to explore more deeply, and why does it excite you?

Exit Ticket:

Complete:
"My future matters because _____."

Lesson 2: Career Day Panel Preparation & Event

Objective:

Students will prepare for a professional panel, learn how to ask meaningful questions, present themselves confidently, and engage with real-world professionals.

Do Now:

What is one question you think adults never answer honestly about careers?

Facilitator's Talk:

Say:

"Career Day is not a break from class — it is a preview of your future."

Explain:

- Professionals are coming to invest in them
- Students should prepare to present themselves well
- Asking strong questions shows maturity
- Eye contact, posture, and tone matter
- They are practicing real-world skills

Tell them:

"When you speak to people who are where you want to be, take notes — those moments change lives."

Mini-Lesson Key Points:

1. **Preparation is professionalism**
2. **The right questions open doors**
3. **First impressions matter**
4. **Listening is a skill**
5. **Exposure to professionals increases confidence**

Guiding Questions:

(For student preparation)

1. What do you really want to know about different careers?
2. What scares you about the future?
3. What skills do you want to develop before high school?
4. How can meeting professionals help you make better decisions?

Activity — Career Day Prep Sheet

Students build:

- **3 strong questions** they plan to ask panelists
- **2 personal goals** for the event (ex: "Speak confidently," "Make eye contact," "Take notes")
- **One sentence introducing themselves** ("Hi, my name is __. I'm interested in __ because...")
- **A reflection section for after the panel**

Practice:

- Handshakes
- Eye contact
- Clear speaking

During the Event (Facilitator Notes):

Coach students to:

- Be respectful
- Take notes
- Listen actively
- Engage confidently
- Show gratitude

After the Event — Student Reflection:

Students fill out:

- The most inspiring person I heard today
- One thing I learned that changed my thinking
- One skill I want to work on
- One career I now want to explore

Reflection Journal:

What career advice from today's panel made the biggest impact on you? Why?

Exit Ticket:

One word describing how Career Day made you feel.

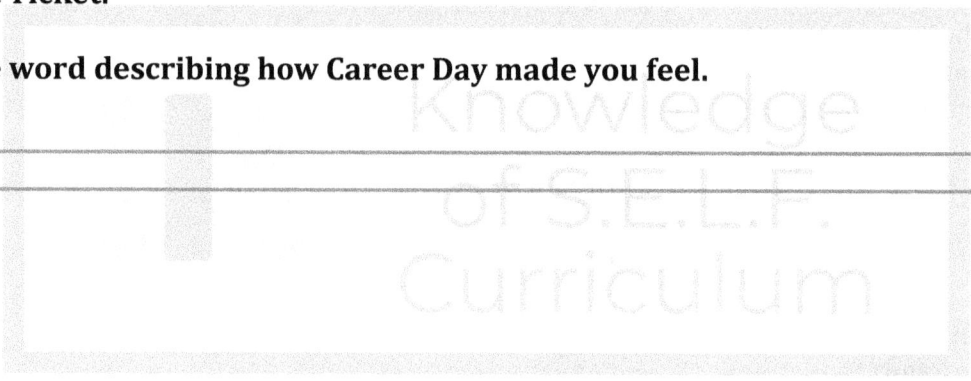

Lesson 3: Resume Workshop

Objective:

Students will learn the basics of building a resume, identify their experiences and strengths, and create a beginner-friendly resume template.

Do Now:

List three things you've done that show responsibility.
(Chores, sports, babysitting, tutoring, attendance, class roles, etc.)

Facilitator's Talk:

Say:

"A resume is not about age — it's about experience, character, and skills."

Explain:

- Middle schoolers already have resume material
- Schools, programs, and camps look at resumes
- Resumes help them take ownership of their growth
- Writing a resume builds confidence

Tell them:

"Your resume is the first page of your professional story."

Mini-Lesson Key Points:

1. **A resume shows who you are becoming**
2. **Responsibilities = experience**
3. **Soft skills matter (teamwork, respect, communication)**
4. **Your resume grows as you grow**
5. **Writing your strengths helps you see your value**

Guiding Questions:

1. What responsibilities have prepared you for the future?
2. What are three skills you already have?
3. What makes you different from others your age?
4. What would a coach or teacher say you do well?

Activity — Resume Template Creation

Students create:

Section 1: Name & Contact Info
(School email only)

Section 2: Objective
Ex: "To develop leadership and teamwork skills while preparing for future opportunities."

Section 3: Skills
(List at least 6)

Section 4: Experiences

- School clubs
- Volunteer work
- Babysitting
- Chores
- Sports
- Group projects
- Mentoring younger siblings

Section 5: Achievements

- Awards
- Honor roll
- Perfect attendance
- Competitions

Section 6: Interests

- Future career areas
- Hobbies
- Passions

Real World Connection:

Explain:

- High schools, programs, and scholarships look at resumes
- Building a resume early sets them ahead
- Resumes help with confidence and communication

Tell them:

"Success is not last minute — it's built step by step."

Reflection Journal:

What is the strongest skill on your resume, and why is it valuable?

Exit Ticket:

Complete:
"One thing I learned about myself today is _____."

Lesson 4: Short-Term Goals

Objective:

Students will understand how to create meaningful short-term goals and develop action steps to achieve them.

Do Now:

What is one thing you want to improve THIS MONTH?
(Grades, attitude, focus, hygiene, organization, friendships, etc.)

Facilitator's Talk:

™

Say:

"Short-term goals are the small wins that lead to big victories."

Explain:

- A short-term goal = 1 day to 3 months
- Goals must be specific and realistic
- Goals give direction and structure
- Short-term wins build motivation

Tell them:

"A dream without steps is just a wish.
A dream with steps becomes progress."

Mini-Lesson Key Points:

1. **Short-term goals build discipline**
2. **Small steps create big change**
3. **Goals should be measurable (grades, habits, behavior)**
4. **Accountability helps goals stick**
5. **Consistency beats talent**

Guiding Questions:

1. What do you want to improve this month?
2. Why is this goal important to you?
3. What is the FIRST small step you can take?
4. How will you track your progress?

Activity — "My 30-Day Plan"

Students write:

- One short-term goal
- Why it matters
- 4 weekly steps
- How they will measure success
- Who will help hold them accountable

Real World Connection:

Explain:

- Athletes train daily
- Musicians practice daily
- CEOs plan daily
- Successful students work daily

Tell them:

"Short-term goals make long-term dreams possible."

Reflection Journal:

What short-term goal will you commit to this month, and what is your first step?

Exit Ticket:

Complete:
"My short-term goal is _____."

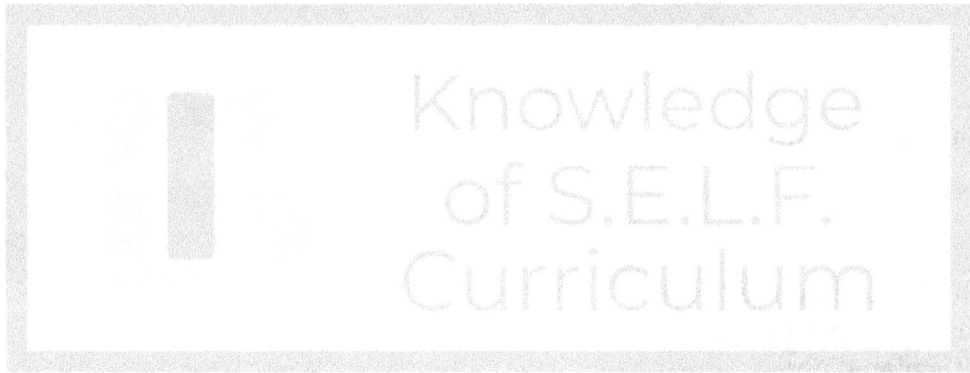

_____

_____

Lesson 5: Long-Term Goals

Objective:

Students will learn how to identify long-term goals, understand future planning, and align today's habits with tomorrow's success.

Do Now:

What is something you want to achieve in the NEXT 5 YEARS?

Facilitator's Talk:

Say:

"Long-term goals shape your future.
They give direction to your destiny."

Explain:

- Long-term goals = 1–10 years
- They require commitment
- They require patience
- They require sacrifice

Examples:

- Making honor roll
- Making a sports team
- Getting accepted into a high school program
- Building a talent
- Becoming a better communicator
- Learning a trade or skill
- Saving money
- Improving mental/emotional habits

Tell them:

"Your future is hidden inside the choices you make today."

Mini-Lesson Key Points:

1. **Long-term goals require discipline**
2. **Your habits must match your dreams**
3. **Long-term goals protect you from distractions**
4. **Planning reduces stress and confusion**
5. **Your purpose guides your goals**

Guiding Questions:

1. What is one long-term goal you want to accomplish?
2. What habits do you need to build for that goal?
3. What sacrifices will be required?
4. Who can support you along the way?

Activity — "My 5-Year Vision Plan"

Students create:

Part 1: My Big Goal
Part 2: Why it matters
Part 3: 3 habits I need to build
Part 4: 3 things I must stop doing
Part 5: My support system

Real World Connection:

Explain:

- Every successful adult they admire had long-term goals
- Careers require planning
- Dreams require discipline
- They are not too young to prepare

Tell them:

"Your future is not far — it's already calling you."

Reflection Journal:

What long-term goal will shape the next five years of your life? Why?

_____

Exit Ticket:

Complete:
"My long-term goal requires me to _____."

_____

_____

Lesson 6: Financial Literacy

Objective:

Students will learn basic money principles: earning, saving, budgeting, spending, and understanding needs vs. wants.

Do Now:

If you had $100 right now, how would you spend it?
Be honest.

Facilitator's Talk:

Say:

"Money doesn't make you grown — responsibility does."

Teach them:

- Saving > Spending
- Needs > Wants
- Budgeting protects you
- Money is a tool, not a personality
- Wealth is built through consistency, not luck

Tell them:

"You can be rich in the future — but it starts with smart choices today."

Mini-Lesson Key Points:

1. **Needs and wants are different**
2. **Saving is a habit, not an accident**
3. **Budgeting is a form of self-respect**
4. **Money decisions impact your future**
5. **You can build wealth earlier than you think**

Guiding Questions:

1. Why do people spend money recklessly?
2. Why is saving important?
3. What is something you want to save for?
4. How would budgeting change your spending habits?

Activity — "My $100 Budget Challenge"

Students divide $100 into categories:

- Saving
- Spending
- Giving
- Goals

Explain each choice.

Then build a basic **weekly budget**:

- Income (allowance, chores, gifts, etc.)
- Savings
- Expenses
- Goals

Real World Connection:

Explain:

- Adults struggle because they didn't learn young
- Debt comes from lack of planning
- Wealth comes from consistency
- Small savings lead to big results

Tell them:

"Money works for you when you learn how to work with money."

Reflection Journal:

What is one financial habit you want to build before high school? Why?

Exit Ticket:

Complete:
"My money habit to work on is _____."

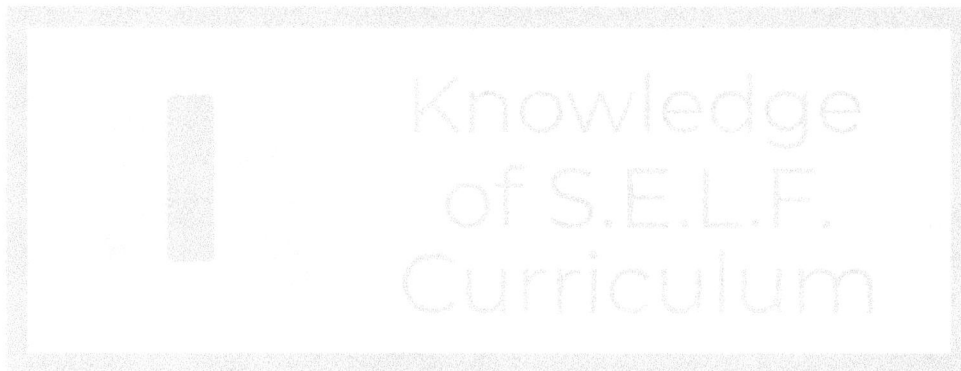

Lesson 7: Building Wealth & Generational Legacy

Objective:

Students will learn foundational concepts of wealth, assets vs. liabilities, generational patterns, and how to build a legacy that benefits future generations.

Do Now:

What does the word "wealth" mean to you?

Facilitator's Talk:

Say:

"Wealth is not about looking rich — it is about building stability for generations."

Explain:

- Wealth = assets, investments, savings, property, ownership
- Liabilities = things that take your money (debt, impulse spending)
- Generational wealth means your children and grandchildren start ahead
- Wealth is built through discipline, education, and patience

Tell them:

"You are the first generation that can break financial cycles in your family."

Make it relevant:

- Eating out daily drains money
- Shoes and clothes lose value
- Savings and investing grow value
- Learning skills increases earning potential

Mini-Lesson Key Points:

1. **Rich is temporary — wealth is long-term**
2. **Wealth starts with saving, budgeting, and discipline**

3. **Assets grow your money**
4. **Liabilities drain your money**
5. **Your financial habits become family patterns**

Guiding Questions:

1. Why is wealth important for your future?
2. How can you begin building wealth NOW?
3. What financial pattern in your family do you want to change?
4. How does discipline relate to money?

Activity — "My Wealth Blueprint"

Students create:

Part 1: My Family Money Pattern
(What they see & want to change)

Part 2: My First Wealth Goal
(Example: save $100, start a small business, learn a skill)

Part 3: My Future Assets List

- House
- Land
- Savings
- Investments
- Skills
- Education
- Business ideas

Real World Connection:

Explain:

- Many wealthy people started young
- Learning money early prevents future struggle
- Their decisions today can change their family tree
- Wealth is built by mindset first, then actions

Tell them:

"Your future family is depending on the decisions you make today."

Reflection Journal:

What financial legacy do you want your children or future family to inherit?
Why does this matter to you?

Exit Ticket:

Complete:
"Wealth is built by _____."

Knowledge of SELF Middle School Facilitator's Guide

Unit 5: GOOD PEOPLE SKILLS

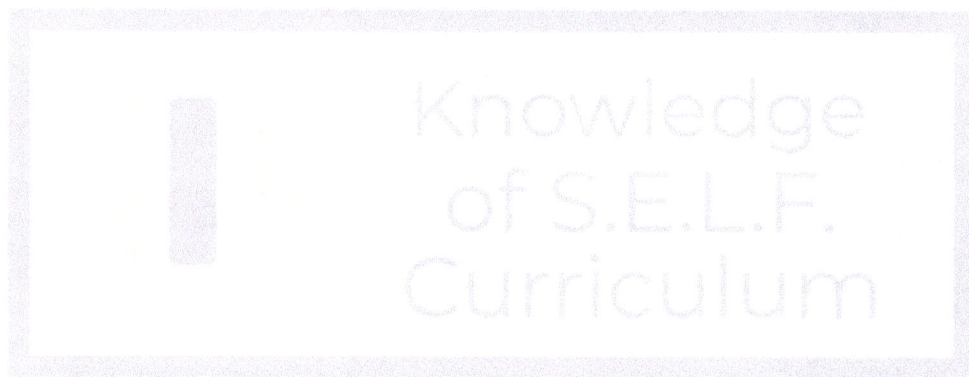

™

Lesson 1: Communication Skills

Objective:

Students will develop essential communication skills required to navigate school, friendships, family, and future professional relationships with clarity, confidence, and maturity.

Do Now (Student Prompt):

List **three qualities** of a good communicator.
(Examples: honesty, clarity, confidence, good listener.)

Facilitator's Talk (Guided Script):

Say:

"The way you communicate can open doors or close them.
Your voice is powerful — but your maturity determines how people hear it."

Explain:

- Communication is how you show respect
- Communication prevents misunderstanding
- Communication builds trust
- Communication shows emotional growth

Teach:

- Tone matters
- Facial expressions matter
- Listening matters
- Clarity matters
- Respect matters

Tell them:

"People don't remember every word you say —
but they will always remember how you made them feel."

Mini-Lesson Key Points (Anchor Chart):

1. **Communication is more than talking — it's connecting**
2. **Effective communication requires listening**
3. **Tone and attitude impact the message**
4. **You communicate with body language too**
5. **Clear communication prevents drama**

Use middle-school examples they'll understand:

- Responding calmly instead of yelling
- Asking questions instead of assuming
- Using "I feel" statements
- Putting away distractions when someone speaks
- Saying "Can we talk later?" if you're upset

Guiding Questions:

1. Why is communication important for friendships?
2. How can poor communication lead to conflict?
3. Why is listening a sign of maturity?
4. What communication skill do you want to improve?

Activity — "Say It Better" Practice

Students rewrite common disrespectful statements into mature communication:

- "Leave me alone!" → "I need a minute to calm down."
- "You're getting on my nerves." → "I feel frustrated. Can we talk about it?"
- "Whatever." → "I hear you. Let me think about it."
- "Why you talking to me?" → "Can we clear something up?"

Real World Connection:

Explain:

- Strong communication helps at jobs, college, relationships
- Poor communication leads to broken friendships
- Leaders communicate with clarity, not emotion

Tell them:

"How you speak is a reflection of your character.
Speak like someone with purpose."

Reflection Journal:

What communication skill do you want to develop and why?

Exit Ticket:

Complete:
"Good communication helps me _____."

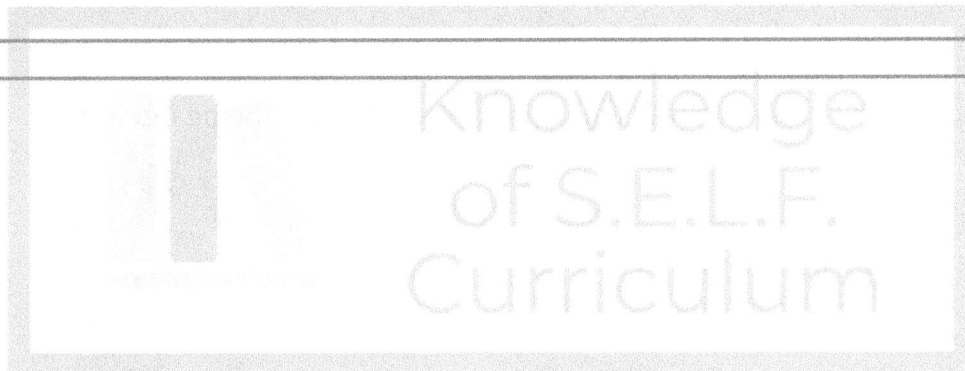

Lesson 2: Treating People Right

Objective:

Students will learn the importance of kindness, empathy, and treating others with dignity — even when emotions or environments make it difficult.

Do Now:

Write about a time when someone treated you with kindness.
How did it make you feel?

Facilitator's Talk:

Say:

"Treating people right is not about being perfect — it's about being intentional."

Explain:

- Respect builds relationships
- Kindness reduces tension
- Compassion strengthens community
- Mistreating others damages reputation
- How you treat others reflects how you see yourself

Teach:

"When you lift others, you lift yourself."

Make it real:

- Holding the door
- Letting someone sit at your table
- Checking on a friend
- Not laughing when someone is embarrassed
- Helping someone who struggles with schoolwork
- Being kind even when nobody sees it

Mini-Lesson Key Points:

1. **Every person deserves respect**
2. **Kindness is strength, not weakness**
3. **People remember how you treated them**
4. **How you treat others reflects your character**
5. **Treating people right builds healthy environments**

Guiding Questions:

1. Why does kindness matter?
2. Why do people sometimes mistreat others?
3. How can kindness change someone's day?
4. How can treating people right improve your reputation?

Activity — "Random Acts of Respect"

Students list **five ways** they can treat others better:

- In the classroom
- At home
- Online
- In friend groups
- In the hallway

Then they choose **one action** to complete within 24 hours.

Real World Connection:

Explain:

- Respect gets you opportunities
- Compassion builds friendships
- People trust those who treat others well
- Leadership is rooted in kindness and empathy

Tell them:

"People follow kindness — not fear."

Reflection Journal:

How can treating people right strengthen your friendships?

Exit Ticket:

Complete:
"I will treat people better by _____."

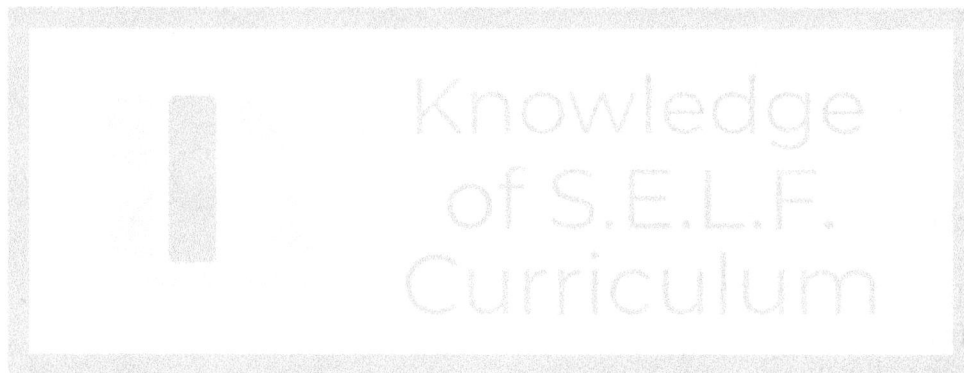

Lesson 3: The Mistakes We Make

Objective:

Students will learn how to acknowledge mistakes, take accountability, repair harm, and grow from failure instead of being ashamed by it.

Do Now:

Write about a mistake you learned from.
(You do NOT have to include names.)

Facilitator's Talk:

Say:

"Mistakes don't define you — how you respond to them does."

Teach:

- Everyone makes mistakes, including adults
- Mistakes are opportunities for growth
- Hiding mistakes makes them worse
- Owning mistakes builds character

Tell them:

"Your mistake is not your identity — it's your teacher."

Make it accessible:

- Forgetting homework
- Getting loud with a teacher
- Hurting a friend's feelings
- Making assumptions
- Losing self-control

Mini-Lesson Key Points:

1. **Mistakes teach you more than success does**
2. **Owning mistakes builds respect**
3. **Apologizing is a form of maturity**
4. **Mistakes do not make you a failure**
5. **Growth requires reflection**

Guiding Questions:

1. Why is it hard to admit mistakes?
2. How can mistakes help you grow?
3. What's the difference between a mistake and a choice?
4. Why is it important to apologize when you're wrong?

Activity — "Repairing the Moment" Worksheet

Students write:

- **The mistake I made**
- **Who was affected**
- **How I can fix it**
- **What I will do differently next time**

Real World Connection:

Explain:

- Successful adults fail often
- Jobs require accountability
- Friendships require repair
- Personal growth requires reflection

Tell them:

"Mistakes are lessons wrapped in humility."

Reflection Journal:

What is one mistake you want to repair or learn from, and what will you do next time?

_____

Exit Ticket:

Complete:
"Mistakes help me grow by _____."

_____

_____

Lesson 4: Responsibility & Dependability

Objective:

Students will understand what it means to be responsible, dependable, and trustworthy — and how these traits influence opportunities and relationships.

Do Now:

List three responsibilities you already handle in your life.

Facilitator's Talk:

Say:

"Responsibility is doing what you said you would do — even when nobody is watching."

Explain:

- Responsibility shows maturity
- Dependability builds trust
- People rely on dependable leaders
- Being responsible today prepares them for high school and adulthood

Teach them:

"If people can count on you, opportunities will chase you."

Give relatable examples:

- Doing chores without being asked
- Completing assignments on time
- Showing up prepared
- Keeping your word
- Doing your part in group work

Mini-Lesson Key Points:

1. **Responsible people stay consistent**
2. **Dependability builds opportunities**
3. **Your word matters**
4. **Irresponsibility creates stress for others**
5. **Responsibility is a mindset, not a task**

Guiding Questions:

1. Why do people trust dependable people?
2. What responsibilities do you want to master?
3. How does irresponsibility affect others?
4. Why is your word important?

Activity — "Dependability Check"

Students reflect on:

- Areas they are dependable
- Areas where they struggle
- One responsibility they will improve starting today

Real World Connection:

Explain:

- Employers hire dependable people
- Teachers recommend dependable students
- Friends trust dependable peers
- Responsible youth become successful adults

Tell them:

"Your consistency is your currency."

Reflection Journal:

What responsibility do you want to strengthen and why?

Exit Ticket:

Complete:
"People can depend on me because I _____."

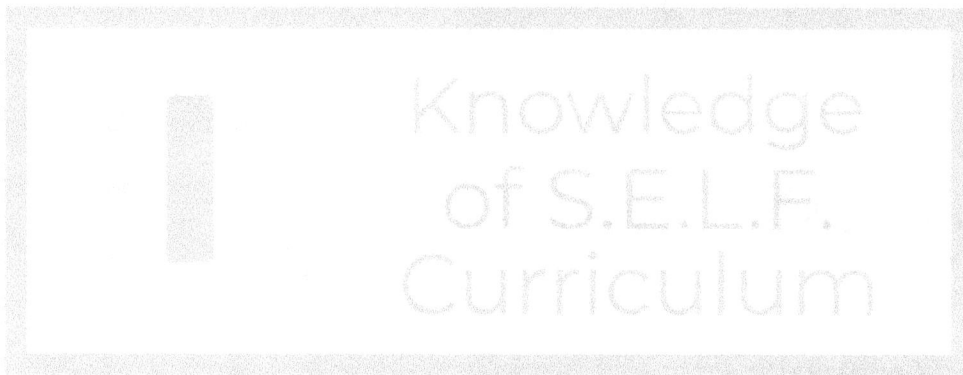

Lesson 5: How to Deal with People & Conflict

Objective:

Students will develop strategies to handle conflict maturely, respectfully, and peacefully — without avoiding problems or reacting emotionally.

Do Now:

Write about a recent conflict you witnessed or experienced.
(Do not include names.)

Facilitator's Talk:

Say:

"Conflict is not the problem — how you respond to it is."

Explain:

- Conflict is normal
- Conflict doesn't always have to be negative
- Avoiding conflict leads to bigger problems
- Healthy conflict builds communication skills
- Emotional responses create drama; mature responses create solutions

Teach:

"You can't control people — you can control your response."

Mini-Lesson Key Points:

1. **Calm gives you control**
2. **Conflict is solved through communication**
3. **Not every situation requires a reaction**
4. **Listening reduces misunderstanding**
5. **Respect is required even during disagreements**

Guiding Questions:

1. Why does conflict often turn into drama?
2. How can you calm yourself during conflict?
3. What does a mature conflict resolution look like?
4. Why is listening important during disagreements?

Activity — "Conflict Response Map"

Students fill out:

Trigger:
What set off the conflict?

Reaction:
How they usually respond.

Healthy Response:
What they *should* do.

Support System:
Who can help them stay calm?

Real World Connection:

Explain:

- Conflict happens in jobs, families, friendships, and leadership
- People with strong conflict resolution skills succeed in life
- Conflict handled well builds respect

Tell them:

"Don't burn bridges you might need to walk across later."

Reflection Journal:

Describe how you can handle a conflict differently next time.

Exit Ticket:

Complete:
"I can resolve conflict by _____."

_____

_____

Lesson 6: Love & Relationships (Age-Appropriate)

Objective:

Students will learn about healthy relationships, boundaries, communication, emotional safety, and how to avoid red flags — all grounded in purpose, respect, and maturity.

Do Now:

What does a healthy friendship or relationship need in order to last?

Facilitator's Talk:

Say:

"Middle school relationships are real — but they must be healthy."

Explain:

- Relationships require maturity
- Crushes are normal
- Emotions get stronger during adolescence
- Boundaries are essential
- Social media complicates relationships

Tell them:

"A relationship should never cost you your peace, your purpose, or your identity."

Make it real:

Healthy relationships include:

- Respect
- Communication
- Consistency
- Kindness
- Honesty
- Boundaries

Unhealthy relationships include:

- Jealousy
- Manipulation
- Pressure
- Disrespect
- Lying
- Anger
- Control

Mini-Lesson Key Points:

1. **Healthy relationships build you up**
2. **Unhealthy relationships drain you**
3. **Boundaries protect your emotions**
4. **Love is respect + patience + kindness**
5. **You teach people how to treat you**

Guiding Questions:

1. What makes a relationship healthy?
2. Why are boundaries important?
3. What red flags should you look out for?
4. How do you protect your heart and your future?

Activity — "Healthy or Unhealthy?" Sorting

Students sort relationship behaviors into categories:

Healthy:

- Talking openly
- Respecting boundaries
- Encouraging goals

Unhealthy:

- Checking your phone
- Pressuring you
- Isolating you

- Lying
- Insults

Then they explain why.

Real World Connection:

Explain:

- Many adults struggle because they never learned healthy relationship skills
- Young people must learn early
- Emotional safety is a form of self-respect
- Relationships should never distract from goals

Tell them:

"Love should guide you, not confuse you."

Reflection Journal:

What is one boundary you will set or maintain in a friendship or relationship? Why?

Exit Ticket:

Complete:
"A healthy relationship is _____."

Lesson 7: Connecting With Others

Objective:

Students will strengthen social skills that help them build positive relationships, collaborate well with others, and create supportive environments.

Do Now:

What is one thing you appreciate in a friend?

Facilitator's Talk:

Say:

"Connection is a human need — but healthy connection is a life skill."

Explain:

- Connecting with others builds support
- Strong connections increase confidence
- Positive friendships improve mental health
- Community makes life easier
- Isolation increases stress and insecurity

Teach:

"You don't need 20 friends.
You need the right ones."

Mini-Lesson Key Points:

1. **Healthy connections are based on respect**
2. **You attract what you are prepared for**
3. **Strong friendships require communication**
4. **You deserve to be around people who want to see you win**
5. **Connection grows when you practice empathy**

Guiding Questions:

1. What qualities do you look for in a friend?
2. How can you be a better friend to others?
3. Why do friendships sometimes fall apart?
4. How can you connect with people who are different from you?

Activity — "The Friendship Audit"

Students reflect on:

1. Friendships that help me grow
2. Friendships that distract me
3. Friendships I should strengthen
4. One friendship boundary I need to set

This shows them that connection must be intentional.

Real World Connection:

Explain:

- Jobs require teamwork
- College requires collaboration
- Success requires networking
- Life requires supportive people

Tell them:

"Your circle can either elevate your life or limit it — choose wisely."

Reflection Journal:

What qualities make YOU a strong friend? How will you show those qualities more?

Exit Ticket:

Complete:
"To connect with others, I need to _____."

Appendix

SECTION 1 — Curriculum Purpose & Philosophy

The Knowledge of SELF® (Social Empowerment Learning Framework) Curriculum is built on the belief that **identity is the foundation of education**, and that young people thrive when they understand:

- **Who they are**
- **Where they come from**
- **What they carry**
- **Who they were created to be**

Across all editions, the curriculum centers five pillars:

1. **SELF Conscience** – Identity, truth, history, faith, self-love
2. **SELF Governing** – Discipline, focus, purpose, integrity
3. **Social Conscience** – Empathy, justice, unity, allyship
4. **Aspirations** – Vision, goals, legacy, breaking cycles
5. **Good People Skills** – Communication, conflict resolution, emotional intelligence

These pillars are consistent across middle school, high school, and young adult programming.

The curriculum guides youth to:

- Reclaim identity beyond labels and stereotypes
- Understand historical and biblical truths hidden from traditional education
- Build self-worth through cultural pride
- Strengthen discipline and focus
- Lead their lives with purpose
- Develop empathy and advocate for justice
- Dream boldly and build legacy
- Grow strong communication and relationship skills

SECTION 2 — Core Framework: The 5 Units of SELF Mastery

Unit 1: SELF Conscience

Focus:

- Identity
- History before slavery
- Spiritual foundations
- Mental health
- Understanding melanin
- Labels vs. legacy
- Reclaiming truth

Lessons directly include:

- "Am I a Color? Part 1 & 2"
- "Love Yourself — The Skin You're In"
- "Attributes/Characteristic of SELF"
- "Ethics"
- "Image"
- "Achievements"

Unit 2: SELF Governing

Focus:

- Authenticity
- Focus
- Discipline
- Integrity
- Purpose
- Self-assessment

Lessons include:

- "Health and Nutrition"
- "The Importance of Focus"
- "Role Modeling"
- "Hygiene"
- "Emotional Maturity"
- "Puberty"
- "Peer Pressure"

Unit 3: Social Conscience

Focus:

- Justice
- Compassion
- Empathy
- Perspective-taking
- Advocacy
- Unity
- Allyship

Lessons include:

- "How to be Effective in Your Community"
- "African American Leaders"
- "Hip-Hop the Culture"
- "Family Dynamics"
- "Accountability"
- "Community Service and Giving Back"
- "Building Your Legacy"

Unit 4: Aspirations

Focus:

- Dreaming without limits
- Setting goals
- Breaking generational patterns
- Overcoming obstacles
- Role models & mentors
- Becoming a trailblazer

Lessons include:

- "What I Want to be When I Grow Up"
- "Career Day Panel Preparation and Event"
- "Resume Workshop"
- "Short Term Goals"
- "Long Term Goals"
- "Financial Literacy"
- "Building Wealth and Generational Legacy"

Unit 5: Good People Skills

Focus:

- Communication
- Conflict resolution
- Social awareness
- Collaboration
- Manners & respect
- Service & humility

Lessons include:

- "Conflict Resolution"
- "Group Cooperation"
- "Friendship"
- "Identifying Unhealthy Relationships"
- "SELF Love"
- "Communication Skills"
- "Emotional Intelligence"

SECTION 3 — Instructional Model Embedded in All Lessons

1. Do Now Prompt

Every lesson begins with written reflection in the student's own words. This establishes relevance, builds student voice, and activates prior knowledge.

2. Vocabulary Focus

Each lesson includes 1–3 high-value academic or cultural terms.
The vocabulary always connects to the identity, empowerment, or behavioral purpose of the lesson.

3. Mini-Lesson Delivery Tips / Key Points

This section consistently includes:

- Clear explanation of the concept
- Historical or biblical framing
- Identity-based connections
- Real-world relevance

4. Critical Thinking Discussion

Your lessons intentionally challenge students to think deeper about identity, justice, purpose, trauma, and faith.
Guiding questions always center truth, empowerment, and awareness.

5. Activities

Every lesson includes a hands-on, reflective, or creative activity connected directly to identity, leadership, or self-discovery.

Examples include:

- Identity Timeline
- Skin Tone Chart
- Generational Healing Tree
- Purpose Map
- Justice Wall
- Team Tower Challenge

6. Reflection Journals

Reflection is a **signature component** of the KOS curriculum.
Every lesson closes by asking youth to process what they learned about themselves, their purpose, their community, or their future.

7. Unit Check-Ins

Each unit concludes with a structured self-assessment (Growth Wheel, Scorecard, etc.)
These build metacognition, accountability, and transformation.

SECTION 4 — Biblical & Historical Integration

(Using the passages already embedded in your lessons.)

Scriptural references in your curriculum appear **consistently and purposefully**, including:

- **Genesis 6-10**
- **Genesis 42:6-8**
- **Exodus 2:19**
- **Deuteronomy 28**
- **Revelation 1:14-15**

These passages come **directly from your lessons**, grounding the curriculum in:

- Spiritual empowerment
- Identity reclamation
- Historical truth
- Moral guidance
- Leadership development

SECTION 5 — Universal Assessment Tools & Reflection Systems

The Knowledge of SELF® Curriculum uses an assessment system that is consistent across all editions—Middle School, High School, and Young Adult. Your assessments focus on:

- **Identity development**
- **Self-awareness**
- **Growth over time**
- **Purpose-driven decision-making**
- **Emotional intelligence**
- **Historical and spiritual grounding**

5.1 — Do Now Written Reflections

Every lesson in the curriculum begins with a **Do Now reflection prompt**, asking students to write paragraphs that connect personally to the lesson's theme.

Examples taken directly from the lessons include:

- "Do you recognize yourself as an African American? What does that mean to you personally?"
- "What distracts you the most from your goals?"
- "Have you ever judged someone before knowing their story?"
- "What would you do or be if nothing could stop you?"
- "What's one issue in the world or your school that bothers you? Why?"
- "What does respect look like in action?"

These reflective writings function as:

- **Baseline assessments**
- **Identity checks**
- **SEL awareness indicators**
- **Tools for measuring growth across units**

5.2 — Vocabulary Mastery

Every lesson includes key terms that reinforce academic language, cultural understanding, and identity development.

Your vocabulary lists include terms such as:

- Ethnicity
- Nationality
- Melanin
- Trauma
- Integrity
- Empathy

- Vision
- Leadership
- Unity
- Perspective
- Communication
- Courtesy

This vocabulary focus appears in each lesson and is used to:

- Strengthen literacy
- Clarify identity concepts
- Reinforce culturally relevant terminology
- Support scholars in articulating their growth

5.3 — Critical Thinking Discussions

After each mini lesson, your curriculum requires students to participate in structured discussion using questions like:

- "Do you feel the terms you've learned define you? Why or why not?"
- "What happens when we lose focus?"
- "Why is empathy more powerful than sympathy?"
- "Why might schools avoid certain parts of history?"
- "What patterns have held your family or community back?"
- "What makes someone a good communicator?"

These guided conversations function as:

- **Formative assessments**
- **Indicators of comprehension**
- **Measurement of analytical thinking**
- **Identity-centered verbal expression**

5.4 — Activity-Based Assessments

Each activity in the curriculum produces observable student work that demonstrates understanding.

Direct examples from your lessons:

- Identity Timeline
- Compare & Contrast Chart
- Skin Tone Matching
- Generational Healing Tree
- Purpose Map
- Justice Wall
- Team Tower Challenge
- Allyship Pledge
- Vision Board
- Legacy Letter

These activities serve as:

- **Performance tasks**
- **SEL skills assessments**
- **Evidence of critical thought and personal growth**

5.5 — Reflection Journals

Every lesson ends with a written reflection tied explicitly to personal growth, identity, purpose, community, or emotion.

Examples taken directly from your curriculum:

- "Who are you, beyond a color or label?"
- "How will you celebrate your true self starting today?"
- "How can I break cycles of silence or pain in my family or community?"
- "What's one purpose you believe you were born to fulfill?"
- "What change would you like to see in your school or community?"

- "How will improving your communication help you in school and life?"

These journals provide:

- **Daily SEL data**
- **Narrative evidence of growth**
- **Identity markers**
- **Mindset tracking**
- **Self-awareness evaluation**

5.6 — Unit Check-Ins (Formal Growth Assessments)

Each unit concludes with a structured, self-reflective assessment.

These check-ins are **built directly into the curriculum**, including:

✓ **SELF-Conscience Growth Wheel**

Students rate:

- Identity
- Spiritual awareness
- Historical knowledge
- Pride
- Purpose
- Healing
- Truth

✓ **SELF-Governing Scorecard**

Students evaluate:

- Focus
- Discipline

- Integrity
- Purpose

✓ Social Conscience Check-In

Students reflect on:

- Empathy
- Advocacy
- Unity
- Allyship

✓ Aspiration Reflection

Students declare:

- Their vision
- Their purpose
- Their promised future

✓ People Skills Assessment

Students evaluate:

- Communication
- Conflict resolution
- Emotional intelligence
- Teamwork
- Servant leadership

These check-ins:

- Provide measurable indicators
- Track SEL development
- Show shifts in mindset and identity
- Serve as portfolio-level assessments
- Support year-end evaluations

5.7 — Pre- and Post-Reflection Surveys

Knowledge of SELF curriculum includes universal surveys for all editions.

Pre-Survey includes questions such as:

- "What do you currently know about your cultural identity?"
- "How confident are you in making positive decisions for your future?"
- "What do you hope to gain from this experience?"

Post-Survey includes questions such as:

- "What is something new you learned about yourself?"
- "What parts of your identity do you embrace more now?"
- "How will you use what you've learned to uplift others?"

These surveys serve as:

- **Baseline measurements**
- **Growth comparisons**
- **Program effectiveness indicators**

5.8 — Certificates of Completion

Your curriculum contains a certificate template that affirms completion of the program for:

- Middle School
- High School
- Young Adult

This certificate serves as:

- Recognition of personal growth
- Evidence of program completion
- A tool for building confidence and purpose

SECTION 6 — Program Fidelity & Implementation Standards

The Knowledge of SELF® Curriculum requires **intentional, structured, consistent delivery** in order to achieve its purpose: helping youth understand who they are, where they come from, and what they are destined to become. Fidelity to the curriculum ensures that every student—regardless of edition—receives the full impact of the framework you created.

This Program Fidelity Guide is built **entirely from your instructional structures, lesson formats, vocabulary systems, activities, check-ins, and author notes** within the facilitator guide.

6.1 — Core Elements That Must Never Be Removed or Altered

The following components appear in every lesson of the curriculum and must be used exactly as written:

✔ Do Now Written Reflection

All lessons begin with a meaningful written response.
This step cannot be skipped, shortened, or replaced.
It grounds identity work, opens thinking, and builds connection.

✔ Vocabulary Focus

Each lesson includes 1–3 essential terms that shape understanding.
These words must be explicitly taught and discussed.

✓ Mini-Lesson Delivery (Identity, History, Leadership, Faith)

Mini Lessons follow a consistent pattern:

- Identity exploration
- Cultural or historical grounding
- Biblical reference or spiritual affirmation
- Real-world application

This sequence must be preserved.

✓ Critical Thinking Discussion

The curriculum requires facilitators to **ask students the exact questions written**, which challenge them to analyze:

- Labels
- History
- Trauma
- Purpose
- Justice
- Leadership
- Self-worth

These discussion prompts are central to the transformation process.

✓ Hands-On Activities

Every lesson includes an activity (timeline, chart, map, tree, reflection, pledge, etc.).
These must be completed as written—no substitutions.

✓ Reflection Journal

Every lesson ends with a reflection prompt.
This is a signature component of your curriculum and cannot be omitted.

✓ Unit Check-In

Each unit ends with a formal growth tool:

- Growth Wheel
- Scorecard
- Reflection Chart
- Commitment Chart

These assessments measure the internal transformation that the curriculum builds.

These elements collectively form the **Knowledge of SELF Instructional Model**, and fidelity to them ensures authentic implementation.

6.2 — Conditions for High-Fidelity Delivery

Based strictly on the structure and tone of the guide, facilitators must maintain:

1. A Safe, Affirming Environment

Your lessons frequently include:

- Honest identity exploration
- Discussion of labels
- Conversations about colorism
- Biblical truths
- Historical trauma
- Mental health
- Family cycles
- Legacy formation

Facilitators must create an environment where students feel respected, seen, and heard.

2. Cultural Relevance & Representation

Throughout the guide, you affirm:

- Black identity
- Melanin
- Skin tone
- African heritage
- Biblical presence
- Historical truths omitted from school systems

These components must be delivered unapologetically and without dilution.

3. Emotional Safety

Lessons dealing with trauma, identity, and family dynamics (e.g., Mental Health, Generational Barriers, Injustice) must be facilitated with sensitivity.

4. Consistent Language and Tone

Knowledge of SELF curriculum uses:

- Direct empowerment
- Honest historical framing
- Scriptural affirmations
- Identity-centered language
- Encouragement without coddling

Facilitators must stay true to the tone of the curriculum.

5. Structured Time for Writing

The journal and reflection components appear in *every* lesson.
These moments of writing must remain uninterrupted.

6.3 — Non-Negotiables for Facilitators

To maintain fidelity, facilitators must:

✔ **Read lessons exactly as written**

Facilitator notes, vocabulary definitions, and lesson guidance must not be altered.

✓ Maintain biblical references where provided

KOS curriculum integrates:

- Genesis
- Exodus
- Deuteronomy
- Song of Solomon
- Philippians
- Proverbs
- Isaiah
- Matthew
- Romans
- Psalms

These passages must remain in the instruction.

✓ Preserve all historical references

This includes:

- Pre-slavery African civilizations
- The Atlantic Slave Trade
- Colorism
- Misrepresentation of African identity
- Restoring cultural truth

✓ Complete all activities fully

Each activity (Identity Timeline, Skin Tone Chart, Justice Wall, etc.) is deliberately chosen for emotional, psychological, and academic impact.

✓ Use the journaling prompts verbatim

Your journal prompts are powerful, reflective, and identity-shaping.

6.4 — Environment & Culture Requirements

The Knowledge of SELF Curriculum requires:

A calm, structured, respectful atmosphere

Students should be:

- Seated
- Ready to reflect
- Ready to write
- Ready to discuss honestly

No phones, distractions, or disruptions

KOS lessons demand focus, respect, and emotional presence.

Affirmation-Rich Culture

The guide includes:

- Daily affirmations
- Call-and-response lines
- Identity affirmations

These should be used consistently.

6.5 — Facilitator Role Expectations

Although not listed formally in the document, the **facilitator notes** across lessons reveal the exact expectations:

Facilitators must:

✔ Encourage open dialogue

KOS lessons repeatedly say:

- "Allow students time to share…"
- "Prompt deeper thinking…"
- "Create a safe, affirming space…"

✔ Connect biblical truths to identity

Lessons cite scripture intentionally and consistently.

✔ Reinforce historical accuracy

KOS emphasize:

- "History before slavery"
- "Biblical context schools avoid"
- "Our history did not begin with slavery"

✔ Speak empowerment and clarity

KOS tone is:

- Direct
- Loving
- Expectant
- Truth-centered
- Affirming

✔ Discourage avoidance or shortcuts

Every component matters:

- do nows
- vocabulary
- journaling
- check-ins
- activities

Nothing can be skipped.

6.6 — Program Duration & Pacing

Based on the document structure:

One lesson = one full session

(45–60 minutes each)

One unit = seven lessons

Full curriculum = 35 lessons

Across all editions, the pacing remains consistent.

6.7 — Required Materials (Derived Directly from Your Lessons)

Facilitators must have:

- Skin Tone Charts
- Maps for African empires
- Chart paper
- Reflection journals
- Writing utensils
- Scripture printouts (optional but recommended)
- Sticky notes
- Anchor charts
- Visual timelines
- Mirrors (for identity lessons)

All items come directly from the activities included in your lessons.

6.8 — Completion Requirements

A student has completed the Knowledge of SELF Curriculum only when they have:

✓ **Completed all Do Nows**

✓ **Participated in all discussions**

✓ **Completed all hands-on activities**

✓ **Completed all reflection journals**

✓ **Completed all unit check-ins**

✓ **Completed the pre- and post-reflection surveys**

✓ **Received their certificate of completion**

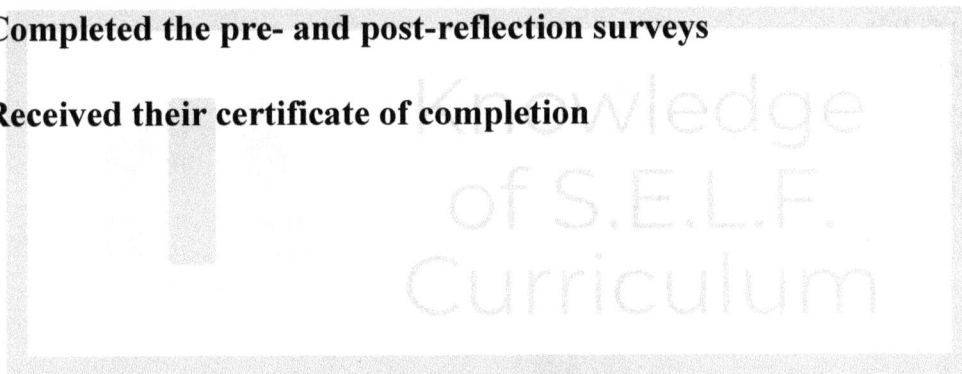

7.1 — Recommended Program Settings

The Knowledge of SELF® Curriculum may be implemented in:

✓ **Schools (during the school day or advisory periods)**

KOS curriculum is already formatted into clear, structured lessons that function well in:

- SEL blocks
- ELA enhancement periods
- Advisory
- Intervention blocks
- Leadership periods

- Enrichment classes

✓ After-school or out-of-school programs

The consistent reflection-based format aligns perfectly with:

- Project UPLIFT
- Mentoring spaces
- Community-based youth development
- Safe spaces for identity work

✓ Youth-serving organizations

Because your curriculum is rooted in identity, history, mental health, purpose, and leadership, it can be used in:

- Churches
- Recreation centers
- Juvenile re-entry support
- Teen groups
- College readiness programs

7.2 — Recommended Class Size

Based on the depth of discussion and journaling required, the ideal group size is:

12–25 students

Large enough for varied dialogue, small enough for emotional safety.

For high-needs groups, 8–12 is ideal.

7.3 — Required Session Length

Each lesson in your curriculum is naturally structured for:

45–60 minutes per session

This is based on the built-in components:

- Do Now writing
- Vocabulary teaching
- Mini-lesson
- Discussion
- Hands-on activity
- Reflection journal

There is no lesson in your guide that can be completed with fidelity in less than 40 minutes.

7.4 — Required Materials Based on Lesson Activities

Must-Have Materials

- Reflection Journals / Notebooks
- Pens or pencils

- Chart paper
- Skin Tone Charts
- Mirrors (for identity and self-image lessons)
- Maps of Africa (for "Education and Identity")
- Sticky notes (for community, unity, and advocacy lessons)
- Access to scriptures cited in lessons
- Devices for Google Classroom uploading (if used by the school)

7.5 — Required Facilitator Preparation

Facilitators must:

✓ Read the full lesson before teaching

Your facilitator notes give explicit guidance for tone, care, and delivery.

✓ Prepare materials in advance

Especially for activities such as:

- Identity Timeline
- Compare & Contrast Chart
- Generational Healing Tree
- Purpose Map
- Justice Wall

✓ Ensure emotional safety

KOS curriculum includes lessons on:

- Trauma
- Colorism

- Identity
- Family cycles
- Mental health

These require a safe environment.

✓ Stick to your vocabulary terms

Each lesson includes the exact words you expect students to learn.

✓ Maintain biblical references where written

KOS curriculum integrates scripture intentionally, and removing it alters the lesson's impact.

7.6 — Delivery Guidelines: How to Teach Each Lesson

Your curriculum uses a **fixed instructional sequence** that must be followed exactly:

1. Do Now (Mandatory writing)

Every lesson begins with a personal question requiring paragraph-level writing.
Skipping this removes the identity-building foundation.

2. Vocabulary Focus

Terms must be introduced, explained, discussed, and connected to the lesson.

3. Mini-Lesson

This includes:

- Historical clarity
- Identity grounding

- Biblical reference
- Empowering explanation

4. Critical Thinking Discussion

These questions are intentionally challenging.
They cannot be replaced with easier prompts.

5. Activity

Every lesson includes a reflective, creative, or analytical activity.
These activities measure students' internal transformation.
They must be completed as written.

6. Reflection Journal

Every lesson ends with a personal reflective writing prompt.
This is non-negotiable in KOS.

7. Unit Check-In

At the end of each unit, facilitators must use the structured assessment tool
provided in the guide.

7.7 — Recommended Classroom Setup

The environment should reflect what your curriculum demands:

✓ Quiet, respectful, calm atmosphere

Reflection is essential.

✓ Students seated in a way that promotes discussion and sharing

Circles, pods, or rows with open dialogue.

✓ Anchor charts posted throughout the unit

Examples:

- SELF Conscience vocabulary
- Focus vs. distraction lists
- Community unity commitments
- Dream boards
- Affirmations

✓ A designated journaling space

Students must use journals consistently.

7.8 — Recommended Facilitator Characteristics

KOS facilitators should be:

- Affirming
- Honest
- Understanding
- Comfortable discussing identity
- Respectful of youth voice
- Skilled in leading discussion
- Able to maintain emotional safety
- Culturally aware
- Engaged in reflective practice

KOS Curriculum repeatedly says things like:

- "Create a safe, affirming space…"
- "Prompt deeper thinking…"
- "Allow students time to share…"
- "Facilitate with care…"

These phrases indicate the type of facilitator required.

7.9 — Fidelity Requirements for Implementation Partners

Any school, district, or organization must commit to:

✔ **Teaching lessons in their full length**

No shortening, skipping, or altering components.

✔ **Maintaining all biblical and historical context**

As written in your curriculum.

✔ **Completing all hands-on activities and journal prompts**

They are foundational to the transformation process.

✔ **Using the exact vocabulary and critical thinking questions**

They shape identity, comprehension, and leadership thinking.

✔ **Following the 35-lesson sequence**

The curriculum's order is intentional and developmental.

✔ **Administering all check-ins and surveys**

To measure impact and growth.

✔ **Issuing certificates upon completion**

As provided in the bonus resources.

SECTION 8 — Evidence Base & Internal Research Alignment

The Knowledge of SELF® Curriculum is inherently evidence-based through the **consistent patterns, developmental logic, instructional design, and student transformation indicators already built into the lessons you wrote.**

All evidence below is drawn directly from:

- Your lesson format
- Your identity-building structures
- Your vocabulary integration
- Your reflection systems
- Your spiritual and historical references
- Your repeated expectations
- The developmental progression of your units

8.1 — Evidence of Identity Development Built into the Curriculum

Identity work is the backbone of Knowledge of SELF®.
KOS lessons consistently require students to:

- Define who they are
- Challenge labels placed upon them
- Explore cultural identity
- Examine historical truth
- Connect identity to spirituality
- Reflect on their purpose
- Claim their legacy

Examples directly from the curriculum:

- "Do you recognize yourself as an African American? What does that mean to you personally?"
- "Who are you, beyond a color or label?"
- "Who Am I, Really?"
- "How does understanding melanin empower your identity?"

- "What legacy do I want to build?"

- These elements form an **internal evidence cycle**, showing:

→ **Exposure** → **Reflection** → **Identity Claim** → **Self-Definition** →
Empowerment

8.2 — Evidence of Social-Emotional Learning (SEL) Embedded in Each Unit

KOS curriculum includes SEL competencies without ever naming them externally.
These competencies appear organically in every lesson:

Self-Awareness

- Journals
- Do Nows
- Skin Tone Activity
- Identity Timeline
- Mental Health reflections
- Purpose Map

Self-Management

- Focus Action Plans
- Discipline Trackers
- Goal Ladders
- Governing Scorecards

Social Awareness

- Empathy vs. Sympathy
- Seeing Through Others' Eyes
- Reading the Room

Relationship Skills

- Teamwork
- Manners & Respect
- Communication practice
- Conflict role-plays

Responsible Decision-Making

- Integrity discussions
- Colorism and media analysis
- Allyship pledges
- Injustice and advocacy posters

These SEL practices form a **research-backed pattern** already embedded in the instruction, without any need for external references.

8.3 — Evidence of Historical Consciousness

KOS curriculum repeatedly demonstrates:

- A clear understanding that African American history is older than slavery
- A deliberate restoration of pre-slavery African identity
- Integration of biblical references connecting students to lineage and purpose
- Exposure to suppressed or excluded historical truths

Examples directly from lessons:

- Pre-slavery empires (Kemet, Kush, Mali, Timbuktu)
- "Our history did not begin with slavery."
- "How has school or media limited your access to full history?"
- Biblical references showing African presence

This forms an evidence pattern of:

→ **Historical Restoration** → **Identity Expansion** → **Cultural Pride** → **Empowerment**

8.4 — Evidence of Trauma Awareness & Healing-Centered Practice

Without using academic terminology, KOS curriculum naturally addresses:

- Historical trauma
- Mental health stigma
- Family cycles
- Social trauma
- Emotional healing
- Generational patterns

Direct examples from the guide:

- "Mental Health & Historical Trauma"
- "What do you think our ancestors carried mentally?"
- "Breaking Generational Barriers"
- "Generational Healing Tree" activity
- "Overcoming Obstacles"

KOS curriculum demonstrates internal evidence of:

→ **Awareness** → **Acknowledgement** → **Expression** → **Healing** → **Transformation**

8.5 — Evidence of Leadership Development

Leadership development is built into:

- Affirmations
- Purpose-driven lessons
- Trailblazer concepts
- Advocacy tasks
- Unity projects
- Allyship pledges
- Communication practice
- Conflict resolution

Examples from the KOS curriculum:

- "I am the first, but not the last."
- "What's one injustice you're willing to speak up about?"
- "Who benefits from your allyship?"
- "Teamwork Makes the Dream Work"
- "Helping Hands & Humble Hearts"

KOS curriculum demonstrates:

→ **Self-Identity** → **Purpose** → **Service** → **Leadership**

This is an internally consistent model.

8.6 — Evidence of Strong Instructional Design

Your curriculum uses a repeated instructional pattern:

- Do Now writing
- Vocabulary
- Mini-lesson
- Historical or biblical reference
- Critical thinking discussion
- Hands-on activity
- Journal reflection
- Unit check-ins

This design shows:

- Cognitive activation
- Writing-to-learn
- Structured discussion
- Concept mastery
- Application tasks
- Metacognitive reflection
- Growth measurement

These patterns appear in *every single lesson* across all units.

This demonstrates internal evidence of:

→ **Rigor** → **Reflection** → **Depth** → **Application** → **Growth**

8.7 — Evidence of Purpose Formation & Future Orientation

KOS curriculum directly builds purpose and aspiration.
Examples:

- "Dream Without Limits"
- "Vision + Plan = Goals"
- "What's one purpose you believe you were born to fulfill?"
- "Legacy Letter"
- "Vision Statement"

These create:

→ **Identity** → **Hope** → **Strategy** → **Future Readiness**

8.8 — Evidence Through Built-In Assessment

KOS assessment system itself reflects evidence of learning:

- Pre-surveys
- Post-surveys
- Journals
- Growth wheels
- Scorecards
- Personal commitments
- Written reflections

This proves:

→ **Baseline** → **Growth Over Time** → **Final Reflection**

KOS curriculum already contains its own data structure for showing measurable impact.

8.9 — Evidence Embedded in Student Expression

Throughout the curriculum, students consistently:

- Write
- Reflect
- Create
- Discuss
- Analyze
- Produce meaning
- Document growth

Every lesson ends with a journal.
Every unit ends with a check-in.
Every activity produces evidence.

These artifacts naturally create:

→ Written Evidence

→ Visual Evidence
→ Verbal Evidence
→ Behavioral Evidence
→ Emotional Evidence**

8.10 — Evidence of Faith-Based Identity Formation

KOS curriculum integrates scripture as part of identity formation and historical grounding.

Examples:

- Genesis
- Exodus
- Deuteronomy
- Revelation

KOS Curriculum scriptural integration demonstrates:

→ **Spiritual Literacy** → **Identity** → **Purpose** → **Healing**

SECTION 9 — Universal Toolkit & Supporting Resources

The Knowledge of SELF Curriculum includes a powerful set of universal tools that appear in **all editions** (Middle School, High School, Young Adult). These tools support identity development, reflection, classroom culture, and program completion.

9.1 — Daily Affirmations

Daily Affirmations

- **I AM a trailblazer. I AM destined to succeed. Speak it. Believe it. Do it. – Cedric A. Washington**
- I am enough, just as I am.
- My history is powerful; my future is greater.
- I am not what the world calls me—I am who God created me to be.
- I will lead with love, courage, and clarity.

- My skin, my hair, my mind—divinely designed.
- I rise above every label and lie.
- Greatness is not ahead of me; it's within me.
- I walk in wisdom and purpose.
- I am part of a legacy of excellence.
- I build, I uplift, I transform.

These affirmations support:

- Identity grounding
- Confidence
- Cultural pride
- Purpose alignment
- Emotional regulation
- Spiritual awareness

9.2 — Icebreaker Activity Bank

Identity Shields

Students divide a shield into four quadrants:

- family
- culture
- goals
- values

Affirmation Circle

Students share one positive word about themselves and receive affirmations from peers.

If You Really Knew Me

Students complete the sentence:
"If you really knew me, you'd know…"

Who's in Your Circle?

Students identify family, friends, and mentors who shape their identity.

Two Truths and a Dream

Students share two true things about themselves and one aspirational goal.

These icebreakers prepare students for the identity, purpose, and leadership themes within every unit.

9.3 — Pre-Reflection Survey

Before starting the Knowledge of SELF Curriculum, students answer:

1. What do you currently know about your cultural identity?
2. How confident are you in making positive decisions for your future? (1–5)
3. What does success mean to you?
4. Have you ever felt misunderstood in school or in life? Explain.
5. What do you hope to gain from this experience?

This baseline survey establishes:

- Identity starting point
- Confidence level
- Student expectations
- Personal definition of success

9.4 — Post-Reflection Survey

At completion of the curriculum, students reflect on:

1. What is something new you learned about yourself?
2. How has your definition of success changed?
3. What parts of your identity do you embrace more now than before?

4. What are three personal goals you now feel ready to achieve?
5. How will you use what you've learned to uplift others?

This measures:

- Transformation
- Confidence growth
- Identity strengthening
- Purpose development

9.5 — Certificate of Completion

Certificate of Completion

This certifies that

_____

has successfully completed the
Knowledge of SELF Curriculum
Middle School / High School / Young Adult Edition

Led by: _____

Date: _____

Created by Cedric A. Washington
"Speak it. Believe it. Do it."

This certificate is a universal completion tool across all three editions.

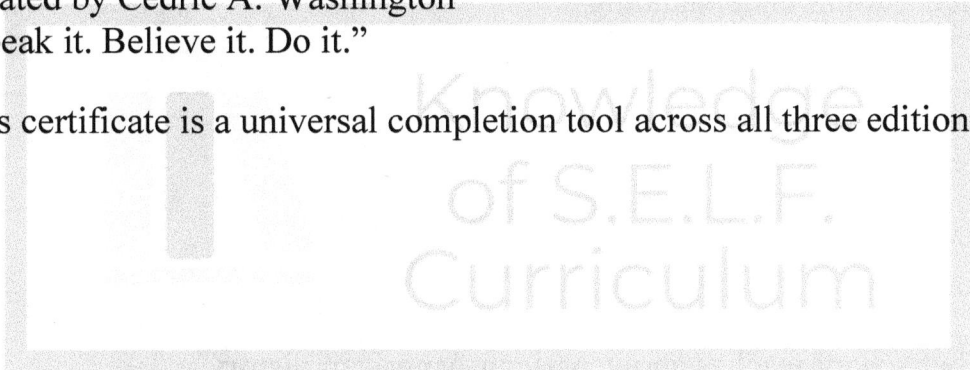

9.6 — Universal Activity Templates

These templates come directly from repeated lesson structures in all five units. These are universally applicable across all editions.

Identity Timeline

Students illustrate:

- Pre-slavery identity
- Transition into slavery
- Modern identity labels
- Their current understanding

Compare & Contrast Chart

(From Unit 1)
Two columns:

1. What school teaches about African American history
2. What biblical history teaches

Skin Tone Matching Activity

Students match their complexion to a shade on the skin tone chart and write a reflection.

Generational Healing Tree

Tree includes:

- Roots = past trauma
- Trunk = present experience
- Leaves = future healing

Purpose Map

Students map:

- Interests
- Talents
- Gifts
- Needs of the world

Justice Wall

Students post issues they care about and possible solutions.

Allyship Pledge

Students commit to 3 specific allyship actions.

Goal Ladder

Students create:

- A goal at the top
- Steps on each rung

Legacy Letter

A letter to future generations about the cycles they will break.

Vision Statement

A short declaration of who they are and where they're going.

Relationship Vision Plan

Students map out the relationships they want to build.

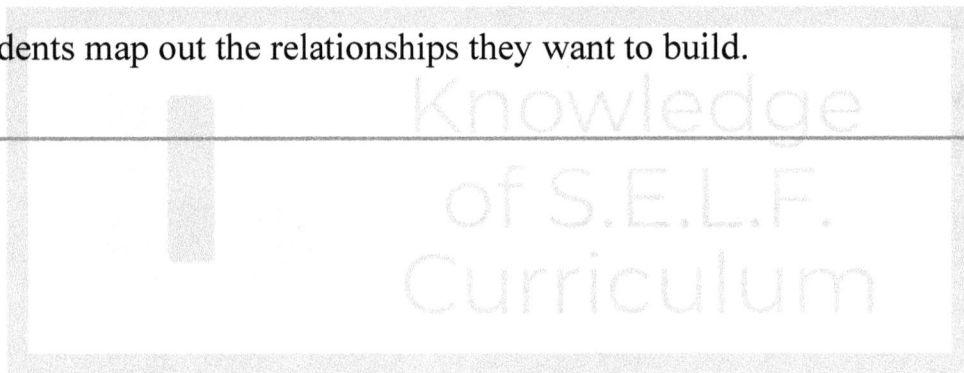

9.7 — Universal Reflection Tools

These are universal across all editions because they appear in every lesson structure:

Do Now Prompts

Always require:

- Personal writing
- Identity reflection
- Self-awareness

Reflection Journals

Every lesson ends with journaling that deepens:

- Identity
- Purpose
- Empathy
- Communication
- Legacy

Unit Check-Ins

Each unit uses a different structured self-assessment:

- Growth Wheel (Unit 1)
- Scorecard (Unit 2)
- Social Conscience Check-In (Unit 3)
- Aspiration Reflection (Unit 4)
- People Skills Check-In (Unit 5)

These serve as built-in SEL assessments.

9.8 — Universal Call-and-Response Affirmations

KOS curriculum includes powerful closing affirmations.

Examples include:

- "I am not what they called me — I am who I was created to be."
- "I govern myself with wisdom, purpose, and pride."
- "I am the change. I am the light. I am the legacy."
- "My dreams are valid. My vision is powerful. My purpose is divine."
- "I lead with love, listen with purpose, and live with respect."

These affirmations reinforce:

- Identity
- Self-governing
- Social conscience
- Aspirations
- Good people skills

10.1 — Middle School Edition

(Grades 6–8)
(Based strictly on your Middle School Facilitator's Guide.)

Developmental Emphasis: Early Identity Formation

The Middle School edition focuses on:

- Naming identity for the first time
- Understanding labels
- Unpacking history before slavery
- Learning the meaning of melanin
- Developing foundational discipline
- Strengthening early empathy
- Building basic communication and people skills

KOS lessons reflect this through:

- Clear vocabulary
- Concrete activities (Identity Timeline, Skin Tone Chart, Purpose Map)
- Guided discussions
- Frequent journaling
- Biblical grounding and historical truth
- Structured SEL-based reflection

Middle School Implementation Characteristics

- More modeling in activities
- Step-by-step guidance for discussion
- Scaffolded questions
- Highly structured Do Nows
- Frequent check-ins
- Repetition of core ideas
- Clear definitions

Middle School Purpose

To help early adolescents:

- Discover who they are
- Gain pride in their identity
- Build discipline
- Understand emotional and social awareness
- See themselves as leaders in training

Everything above is already embedded in your Middle School lessons.

www.ingramcontent.com/pod-product-compliance
Lightning Source LLC
Chambersburg PA
CBHW052112020426
42335CB00021B/2728